Grade 1

Gifted & Talented™

Reading, Writing & Math

Cover Illustration by Mark Stephens
Written by Tracy Masonis and Vicky Shiotsu

Spark Publishing

Dear Parents,

Gifted & Talented Reading, Writing & Math has been designed specifically to promote development of analytic thinking, language arts, and math skills. The activities in this book use a variety of critical strategies, including activities to spark your child's imagination, encourage brainstorming, and sharpen math skills.

The activities are intended to help develop reading, writing, and math skills that your child will use at school and home. Most of the activities can be completed directly on the workbook pages. In some instances, though, your child might like to use a separate sheet of paper to interpret what has been read or work out math problems.

While working in this book, your child may be inspired to create his or her own story or math problems. If so, have your child present his or her work and explain the strategies to you. Praise your child's efforts, and encourage him or her to continue creating them. This type of activity not only stimulates creativity and independent thinking, but also deepens your child's love of learning.

© 2007 by Spark Publishing
Adapted from *Gifted & Talented® Reading, Writing & Math Grade 1*
© 2003 School Specialty Children's Publishing. Published by Gifted & Talented®, an imprint of School Specialty Children's Publishing, a member of the School Specialty Family.

Flash Kids is a registered trademark of SparkNotes LLC

Spark Publishing
A Division of Barnes & Noble
120 Fifth Avenue
New York, NY 10011
www.sparknotes.com

ISBN-13: 978-1-4114-9557-9
ISBN-10: 1-4114-9557-8

For more information, please visit *www.flashkidsbooks.com*
Please submit changes or report errors to *www.flashkidsbooks.com/errors*

Printed and bound in China

10 9 8 7

Table of Contents—Reading

Knowing the Words/Vocabulary/Language Development

Synonyms . . . . We're the Same! 9
Synonyms . . . . Synonym Squares! 10
Synonyms . . . . Take My Place 11

Antonyms . . . . Antonym Artists! 12
Antonyms . . . . Oops! It's Opposite Day! 13
Antonyms . . . . Antonyms Are Opposites! 14

Multiple Meanings . . . . Batty Bats! 15
Multiple Meanings . . . . Match That Meaning! 16
Multiple Meanings . . . . Match That Meaning! 17

Commonly Misused Words . . . . . Common Corrections 18
Commonly Misused Words . . . . . Common Corrections 19

Context Clues . . . . Caitlin Uses Context Clues 20
Context Clues . . . . Caitlin Uses More Context Clues 21
Context Clues . . . . Carlo's Context Clues 22
Context Clues . . . . Carlo's Context Clues Continued 23

Elements of Stories

Character Analysis . . . . What Is a Character? 24
Character Analysis . . . . Character Continued 25
Character Analysis . . . . Character Interview—Lights! Camera! Action! . . 26

Setting . . . . Setting—Place 27
Setting . . . . Setting—Place 28
Setting . . . . Setting—Time 29

Character, Setting, Events . . . . . . Make a Map! 30
Character, Setting, Events . . . . . . Extra! Extra! Read All About It! 31
Character, Setting, Events . . . . . . Extra! Extra! Read All About It! 32

Nonfiction . . . . Fiction or Nonfiction? 33
Nonfiction . . . . Fiction or Nonfiction? 34

Reading Comprehension

Sequencing . . . . Sequencing Pictures 35
Sequencing . . . . Sequencing Patterns 36

Sequencing . . . . Sequencing Riddles 37
Sequencing . . . . Story Time 38

Main Idea . . . . Hey! What's the Big Idea? 39
Main Idea . . . . Picture This! 40
Main Idea . . . . Picture This! 41
Main Idea . . . . What's the Main Idea? 42
Main Idea . . . . Story Time 43

Recognizing Details . . . . What's Missing? 44
Recognizing Details . . . . The Pet Shop 45

Main Idea vs. Details . . . . Highlight Happy! 46
Main Idea vs. Details . . . . Sally's Snake 47

Cause & Effect . . . . What Is Cause and Effect? 48
Cause & Effect . . . . More Cause and Effect! 49
Cause & Effect . . . . We Go Together! 50
Cause & Effect . . . . What Happened? 51

Making Inferences . . . . Inside Out! 52
Making Inferences . . . . Books for Gabby! 53
Making Inferences . . . . Use Your Head! 54
Making Inferences . . . . Where Do I Go? 55
Making Inferences . . . . Help Hattie! 56

Predicting Outcomes . . . . What Will Happen Next? 57
Predicting Outcomes . . . . What's Next? 58
Predicting Outcomes . . . . What Happens Next? 59

Following Directions . . . . Following Directions—Animal Riddles 60
Following Directions . . . . Finding Mistakes—Tricky Triplets 61
Following Directions . . . . Stop Making Sense! 62
Following Directions . . . . Costume Jamboree! 63

Just for Fun . . . . Story Mix-Up! 64
Just for Fun . . . . Just for Fun! 65
Just for Fun . . . . What Can I Make? 66

Reading Answer Key 183–184

Table of Contents—Writing

Writing Words

Naming Words—Nouns . . . . What is a noun? 67
Naming Words—Nouns . . . . Write the nouns 68
Naming Words—Nouns . . . . Fill in the nouns 69
Action Words—Verbs . . . . What is a verb? 70
Action Words—Verbs . . . . Fill in the verbs 71
Describing Words—Adjectives . . . . What is an adjective? 72
Describing Words—Adjectives . . . . Fill in the blanks 73
Just Me! . . . . Just me exercise 74

Writing Sentences

Sentences—Complete Thoughts . . . . . . Writing a sentence 75
Punctuation—Periods . . . . Add the periods 76
Punctuation—Question Marks . . . . Add the question marks 77
Capital Letters Rule! . . . . Rules of capitalization 78
Capital Letters Rule! . . . . Add the capital letters 79

Sentence Starters

Sentence Starters . . . . Finish the sentence 80
Sentence Starters . . . . Finish the sentence 81
Sentence Endings . . . . Begin the sentence 82
Sentence Endings . . . . Begin the sentence 83

Writing Stories

Sequencing . . . . Pictures in order 84
Sequencing . . . . Pictures in order 85
Sequencing . . . . Blank cutting page 86
Beginning, Middle, and End . . . . Sentences in order 87
Beginning, Middle, and End . . . . Sentences in order/Draw a Picture 88
Order Words . . . . First, next, and last 89
Using Order Words . . . . Circle the order words 90
Using Order Words . . . . Write the order words 91
Endings . . . . "African Safari!" 92
Endings . . . . "Kids in Space!" 93
Beginnings and Middles . . . . "The Rickety Roller-Coaster!" 94
Beginnings and Middles . . . . "Gilbert the Tap-Dancing Horse!" 95

Change the Story . . . . "Snow White" 96
Change the Story . . . . "Pinocchio" 97
Follow the Pictures . . . . Rainbow Picnic! 98
Follow the Pictures . . . . Puppy Surprise! 99

More Stories

Brainstorming . . . . Brainstorm 100
Narrowing Your Idea . . . . Write story using list 101
Brainstorming . . . . Brainstorm list 102
Narrowing Your Idea . . . . Write story using list 103
Story Beginnings . . . . "Amazon Adventure!" 104
Story Beginnings . . . . "Candy Land Sleepover!" 105
Story Middles . . . . "A Whale of a Birthday!" 106
Story Middles . . . . "Tick Tock Todd!" 107
Story Endings . . . . "Sleeping Shoes!" 108
Story Endings . . . . "Elaine's Bubble Gum Inventions!" 109
Bringing It All Together . . . . "Upside-Down Morning!" list 110
Bringing It All Together . . . . "Upside-Down Morning!" story 111
Making It Better—Describing Words . . . Using adjectives 112
Making It Better—Describing Words . . . Describe the pictures 113
Proofreading—Punctuation . . . . Symbols and examples 114
Proofreading—Punctuation . . . . Fix the sentences 115
Final Draft—With Illustration! . . . . "Upside-Down Morning!" 116
Final Draft—With Illustration! . . . . "Upside-Down Morning!" 117
Three Things You Like About Your Story! 118
Three Things Someone Else Likes About Your Story! 119
Write a Friendly Letter . . . . Parts of a friendly letter 120
Write a Letter Describing Your Story . . . Your turn 121
Just for Fun! . . . . Funny words! 122
Just for Fun! . . . . Draw and write 123
Just for Fun! . . . . Fun with words! 124
Just for Fun! . . . . Draw and write 125

Writing Answer Key 185

Table of Contents—Math

Number Sense

Spilled Numbers 127
Order, Order! 128
On the Road 129
Who's Who? 130
Mouse and Cheese 131
Flying Home 132
Cooking Up Numbers 133
Mystery Numbers 134–135

Operations and Computations

What's in the Hat? 136
Make Them Equal 137
Find and Circle 138
Sums to 12 139
Juggling Fun 140
High-Flying Numbers 141
Party Time 142

Patterns

Frankie Frog 143
All Aboard! 144
Caterpillar Patterns 145
Dots and Lines 146
Shape Patterns 147

Money

Piggy Bank Riddles 148
Make 25 Cents 149
Coin Patterns 150
A Toy Sale 151
At the Balloon Shop 152

Logical Thinking

A Flower Garden 153
Toy Bunnies 154
Four Dinosaurs 155

Four Brothers 156
Taking a Trip 157
Eager Beaver 158
Sorting Shapes 159
Circus Fun 160
Which Clown? 161
Roger's Triangles 162
How Many Cookies? 163
Library Lineup 164

Measurement
To the Doghouse 165
Paper Caterpillars 166
Heavier or Lighter? 167
Ounces or Pounds? 168
How Much Time Does It Take? 169

Geometry
Shape Puzzles 170
Shape Designs 171
Hidden Squares 172
How Many Triangles? 173
Paper Cutouts 174
Shape Search 175
Robot Riddles 176
What's on the Bottom? 177
Color and Count 178

Statistics and Probability
Cool Scoops 179
Benny's Outfits 180
Jenny's Outfits 181
Goldfish Pets 182

Math Answer Key 186–189

We're the Same!

Words that mean the **same** thing, or close to the same thing, are called **synonyms**.

Write a word from the Word List that has the same meaning as each word below.

Word List			
bright	hop	dad	fast
pretty	plate	silly	center

 sunny

_____

 beautiful

_____

 middle

_____

 dish

_____

 quick

_____

 jump

_____

 goofy

_____

 father

_____

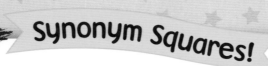

Synonym Squares!

Circle the **synonym** in each square that has the same meaning or close to the same meaning as the word in **bold** print.

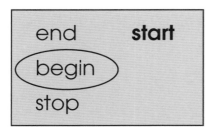
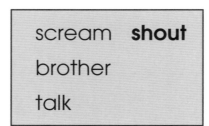
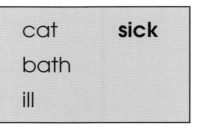

Think of a synonym for each of the three listed words. Then write a sentence using **both** words in your sentence.

smart/_____

_____

_____

bad/_____

_____

_____

little/_____

_____

_____

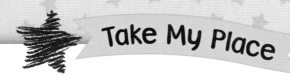

Take My Place

Choose the word from the Word List below that could take the place of the underlined word in each sentence. Write it on the line.

Word List		
pick	tired	cut
porch	pull	bag

I was so <u>sleepy</u>! I couldn't wait to go to bed! _____

Please put all your books in this <u>sack</u>.

_____

Please <u>choose</u> a present you would like to open. _____

Are you strong enough to <u>drag</u> this heavy crate? _____

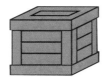

"It is important to <u>trim</u> the extra fabric on your art project," said my art teacher.

_____

We sipped lemonade on the <u>deck</u>.

_____

Antonym Artists!

Name _____

Antonyms are words that have **opposite** meanings. Abby and Abe are Antonym Artists! They like to draw opposite pictures. Help Abe draw the opposite of Abby's pictures.

Oops! It's Opposite Day!

Name _____

Oppie woke up early one morning to discover it was Opposite Day! Everything was opposite! Oppie got dressed, and all his clothes went on backwards! Help Oppie by circling the word in each row that has the opposite meaning of the first word.

pull	push	pillow	grab
fast	burger	danger	slow
thin	fat	tall	skinny
break	fix	hold	glue
harm	ham	cold	help
winter	february	summer	fall
loser	bad	teacher	winner

Antonyms Are Opposites!

Words with **opposite** meanings are called **antonyms**. Circle an antonym for the underlined word in each sentence.

The sky was very <u>dark</u>.   purple   old   light

Turn <u>left</u> at the light.   right   sideways   yellow

The shelf was very <u>high</u>.   pretty   low   loud

The turtle walked <u>slowly</u>.   silly   quickly   nicely

I <u>whispered</u> at the circus.   laughed   coughed   shouted

Bobby is an <u>adult</u>.   child   fan   principal

The clown was very <u>strong</u>.   weak   silly   hungry

The library is a <u>quiet</u> place.   fun   messy   noisy

Batty Bats!

Some words have more than one meaning.

The word *bat* has more than one meaning.

Look at the words and their meanings below. Next to each picture, write the letter that has the correct meaning.

can: A) a metal container
B) to know how

___   ___

band: A) a group of musicians
B) a strip of material

___   ___

cap: A) a soft hat with a visor
B) lid or cover

___   ___

crow: A) a large black bird
B) the loud cry of a rooster

___   ___

Match That Meaning!

Some words have more than one meaning. Look at the list of words. Match the word's correct meaning to the pictures below.

cross: A) to draw a line through
               B) angry

fall: C) the season between summer and winter
             D) to trip or stumble

land: E) to bring to a stop or rest
              F) the ground

_____   _____   _____

_____   _____   _____

Match That Meaning!

The word *may* has more than one meaning.

May or   A) the fifth month of the year
may: B) to be permitted or allowed
                    to do something

May I please get a drink of water?

MAY						
Sunday	Monday	Tuesday	Wednesday	Thursday	Friday	Saturday
			1	2	3	4
5	6	7	8	9	10	11
12	13	14	15	16	17	18
19	20	21	22	23	24	25
26	27	28	29	30	31	

Write the letter of the correct meaning in each blank.

My dad's birthday is in _____.

_____ I please go to the gym?

Many flowers bloom in _____.

Mother, _____ I go to the swimming party?

My brother will come home from college in _____.

Common Corrections

Some words look and sound very much alike, but have very different meanings. For example, make sure you ask for an extra piece of *dessert*, not *desert*!

Look at the words and meanings below.
Write the correct word to complete each sentence.

dessert   **desert**

quiet: not noisy
quite: very

Shhhh, please be _____ in the library.

The turkey was _____ good.

freight: cargo
fright: sudden fear

The ship carried a lot of _____.

The loud noise gave me a sudden _____.

lose: misplace
loose: not tight

My front tooth was _____.

Did you _____ your homework?

Common Corrections

Some words look and sound very much alike, but have very different meanings. Look at the words and meanings below. Write the correct word to complete each sentence.

couch: a sofa
coach: someone who trains athletes

I fell asleep on the _____.

The _____ gave the football team a pep talk.

picture: a visual representation
pitcher: a container for liquids

We hung the _____ in the kitchen.

"Please pass the _____ lemonade," I said.

guessed: made a guess
guest: visitor

I was a _____ in their house.

He _____ the answer and got it right!

Caitlin Uses Context Clues

When you read, it is important to know about context clues. **Context clues** can help you figure out the meaning of a word or a missing word just by looking at the **other words** in the sentence.

Read each sentence below. Circle the context clues, or other words in the sentence that give you hints about the meaning. Choose the answer that fits in each blank. Write it on the line.

It was so (hot) outside that I decided I would go to the (beach) and _____**swim**_____.

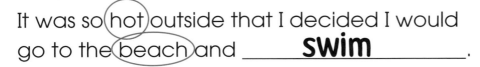

   A) play   B) laugh   C) shovel   D) swim

D) is the correct answer because of the context clues <u>hot</u> and <u>beach</u>. Now you try.

Last night I went to bed very late and now I feel _____.

   A) happy   B) hungry   C) tired   D) yawn

When I broke my mom's favorite vase she was _____.

   A) worried   B) nice   C) magic   D) angry

The clown looked very _____ wearing a tiny pink tutu!

   A) silly   B) smart   C) orange   D) light

Name _____

Caitlin Uses More Context Clues

When you read, it is important to know about context clues. **Context clues** can help you figure out the missing word in a sentence, just by looking at the **other words** in the sentence.

Read each sentence below. Circle the context clues. Choose the answer that fits in each blank. Write it on the line.

The cold wind and lack of heat made me wish I had an extra _____.

    A) umbrella   B) toy   C) shovel   D) jacket

A whale is a very _____ mammal. Sailors often thought whales were actually small islands!

    A) small   B) graceful   C) large   D) blue

Eating fruit is important for _____ health. Fruit is full of many important vitamins.

    A) bad   B) good   C) okay   D) cat

The bus was very large and had a lot of seats. It could carry _____ people.

    A) few   B) hungry   C) many   D) tired

Name _____

Carlo's Context Clues

Context clues can help you figure out the meaning of a word just by looking at the **other words** in the sentence.

Read each sentence below. Circle the context clues. Choose a word from the Word List to replace each word in **bold**. Write it on the line.

Word List		
stop	shined	tease
smart	lively	yummy

This prize-winning chocolate cream pie is **delicious**. _____

Please do not **taunt** your younger brother. Mean words hurt his feelings. _____

The police officer told us to **halt** when we came to the red traffic light. _____

The bouncy, happy puppy was very **energetic**. _____

The silver bowl really **gleamed** after you polished it. _____

The **intelligent** girl always got 100's on her spelling tests. _____

Carlo's Context Clues Continued

Context clues can help you figure out the meaning of a word just by looking at the **other words** in the sentence.

Read each sentence below. Circle the context clues. Choose a word from the Word List to replace each word in **bold**. Write it on the line.

Word List		
petted	understand	tell
little	yelled	

"Don't **reveal** the secret! We want the party to be a surprise!" said Mary. _____

I can't **grasp** that hard math problem! It is too difficult. _____

The baby bird was so **tiny** that we could hardly see it. _____

We **stroked** the soft kitten and heard it purr. _____

The crowd **hollered** when the player was called out. _____

What Is a Character?

A **character** is the **person, animal**, or **object** that a story is about. You can't have a story without a character.

Characters are usually people, but sometimes they can be animals, aliens (!), or even objects that come to life. You can have many characters in a story.

Read the story below and then answer the questions about the main character on the next page.

Jumpin' Jack!

Everybody liked Jumpin' Jack. He was the nicest rabbit in the forest. If he found a carrot, he would split it in half and share it with you. If the baby bunnies were having trouble with their jumps, Jumpin' Jack would patiently help them practice.

Jumpin' Jack had two pointy white ears, a black body, and four white feet that looked like socks. He was very handsome!

The End

First, authors must decide who their main character is going to be. Next, they must decide what their main character looks like. Then, they reveal their character's personality by **what** their character does.

Who is the main character in "Jumpin' Jack!"?

_____

What does Jumpin' Jack look like? Describe his appearance.

_____

_____

Give two examples of what Jumpin' Jack **does** that show that he is kind: _____

_____

_____

Would you want Jumpin' Jack as a friend? Why or why not?

_____

_____

_____

Character Interview—Lights! Camera! Action!

An **interview** takes place between two people, usually a reporter and another person. The interviewer asks questions for the person to answer.

Pretend that you are a reporter. Choose a character from a book you read. If you could ask the character anything you wanted to, what would you ask?

Make a **list of questions** you would like to ask your character:

1. _____

2. _____

3. _____

4. _____

Now pretend your character has come to life and could **answer your questions**. Write what you think he, she, or it would say:

1. _____

2. _____

3. _____

4. _____

Setting—Place

Every story has a **setting**. The setting is the **place** where the story happens. Think of a place that you know well. It could be your room, your kitchen, your backyard, your classroom, or an imaginary place.

Brainstorm some words and ideas about that place. Think about what you see, hear, smell, taste, or feel in that place.

Brainstorm your ideas for a setting below:

_____

_____

_____

_____

see   hear   smell

taste   touch

_____

_____

_____

_____

_____

Where are we? _____

Setting—Place

Read the story below and answer the questions about the setting.

Desert Life

Living in the desert with my family wasn't easy. It was very hot during the day and cold at night. The ground was so dry we couldn't plant a garden or have a front yard with grass. We didn't have trees to climb either, but we did have lots of cacti!

What is the temperature like in the desert? _____

If you were going to visit the desert, what clothes would you take?

_____

_____

Could you plant a garden in the desert? Why or why not?

_____

_____

Are there trees for kids to climb in the desert? _____

Setting—Time

The **setting** is the **place** where the story happens. The setting is also the **time** in which the story happens. A reader needs to know **when** the story is happening. Does it take place at night? On a sunny day? In the future? During the winter?

Time can be:

time of day   a holiday   a season of the year

a time in history   a time in the future

Read the following story. Then answer the questions below.

 **Pancake Mornings**

In the summer, I look forward to Sunday mornings. On Sundays, my parents get up extra early. My mom mixes pancake batter with ripe blueberries, and my dad plays the fiddle. When my brother and I come downstairs for breakfast, the pancakes are on the griddle and my dad is dancing!

On what day of the week does this story take place?

_____

What season is it in this story?_____

What time of day is it?_____

Make a Map!

In a story or book you read, the character or characters may have taken a journey or simply walked around their town. Where did the main events in the story take place? Create a detailed map showing the place where the characters lived. You may wish to ask an adult for help.

1. Draw the outline of your map on a sheet of paper.

2. Be sure to write the title and the author of the book at the top of the map.

3. Think about what places you want to include on your map and draw them.

4. Label the important places, adding a short sentence about what happened there.

5. Add color and details.

6. Share your map with friends and tell them about the story you read.

Extra! Extra! Read All About It!

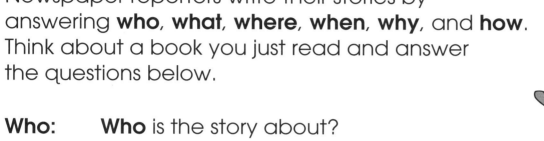

Newspaper reporters have very important jobs. They have to catch a reader's attention and at the same time **tell the facts**.

Newspaper reporters write their stories by answering **who**, **what**, **where**, **when**, **why**, and **how**. Think about a book you just read and answer the questions below.

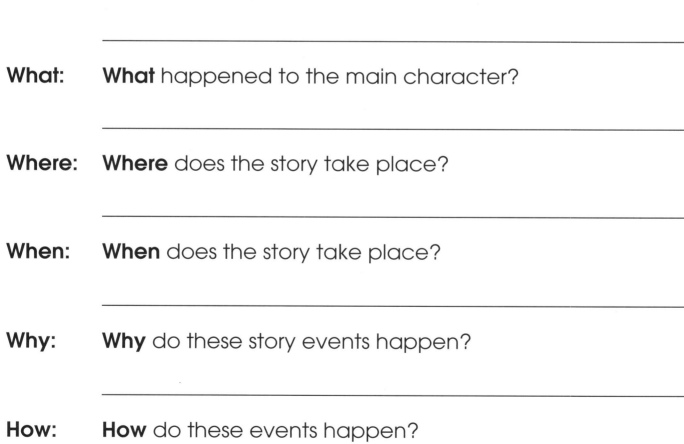

Who: **Who** is the story about?

_____

What: **What** happened to the main character?

_____

Where: **Where** does the story take place?

_____

When: **When** does the story take place?

_____

Why: **Why** do these story events happen?

_____

How: **How** do these events happen?

_____

Extra! Extra! Read All About It!

Use your answers on page 31 to write a newspaper article about the book you read.

BIG CITY TIMES

Title

_____

(Write a catchy title for your article)

_____

_____

_____

_____

_____

_____

_____

_____

Name _____

Fiction or Nonfiction?

Some stories are made up and some are true. **Fiction** stories are made up and **nonfiction** stories are true.

Read the passages below. Then write if they are **fiction** or **nonfiction**.

George Washington was the first president of the United States. The city of Washington, D.C., is named after him.

_____

Taddy Bear loved honey. He would always go with his mom to the Bargain Bear Grocery Store. She would let him fill up their grocery cart with lots of honey pots!

_____

There are fifty states that make up the United States of America. If you put the fifty states in order alphabetically, the first state would be Alabama and the last state would be Wyoming.

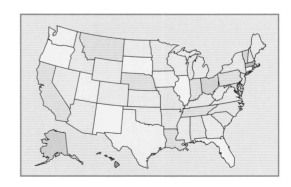

_____

Fiction or Nonfiction?

Some stories are made up and some are true. **Fiction** stories are made up and **nonfiction** stories are true.

"Could it be true?"

"No way. It's just a made-up story!"

Read the passages below. Then write if they are **fiction** or **nonfiction**.

Last night, I was invited to Kazam the Magician's house for dinner. I love to visit his house. We always have cotton candy soup and bubble gum soda for dinner. Then we jump into a tub of vanilla ice cream for dessert. I wish dinner was like this at my house!

_____

Rhode Island is the smallest state in the United States. Its nickname is "The Ocean State." It is a very popular place for families to take summer vacations because it has many beautiful beaches.

_____

Sequencing Pictures

Put the pictures in each column in order. Write **1**, **2**, or **3** next to each picture.

Sequencing Patterns

Look for a pattern of shapes inside each pencil. Choose a shape from the Picture Bank and draw what comes next on each pencil. Then write the name of the shape on the line.

Picture Bank

_____

_____

_____

_____

_____

Sequencing Riddles

To solve the riddles below, look at the letter underneath each line. Next, write the letter that comes **before** each letter.

How do you catch a squirrel?

___ ___ ___ ___ ___   ___ ___   ___   ___ ___ ___ ___
D M J N C   V Q   B   U S F F

___ ___ ___   ___ ___ ___   ___ ___ ___ ___   ___   ___ ___ ___ .
B O E   B D U   M J L F   B   O V U

What has four wheels and flies?

___   ___ ___ ___ ___ ___ ___ ___
B   H B S C B H F

___ ___ ___ ___ ___
U S V D L

Why did the boy run around his bed?

___ ___   ___ ___ ___ ___ ___   ___ ___   ___ ___
U P   D B U D I   V Q   P O

___ ___ ___   ___ ___ ___ ___ ___
I J T   T M F F Q

Name _____

Story Time

Write each group of sentences in the correct order.

My cat was full and went to sleep.   My cat was hungry.
I filled a bowl with cat food.

1. _____

2. _____

3. _____

I got a gold star.   I studied for my spelling test.
My teacher gave us a list of spelling words.

1. _____

2. _____

3. _____

Hey! What's the Big Idea?

Circle the words that are shown in the picture above.

bowl	spatula	bed	dog	ink
oven	pan	jar	pot	phone
mixer	napkins	scooter	girl	sneakers
mitt	paper towels	car	socks	cupcake tin
spoon		cat	milk	

Circle and write the best title for the picture.

Baking With Dad   Chocolate Attack!   Eating Food

_____

Tell why the other two titles are not as good.

_____

_____

Look at the picture. Circle and write the best title on the lines below.

B-r-r-r, It's Cold!   Bears and Birds

Asleep for the Winter   Bears Go Shopping

_____

_____

Fishing   Our New Fish

The Pet Store   Fish and Chips

_____

_____

Spring Cleaning   My New Toy

Saturday Fun   New Shoes

_____

_____

Picture This!

Name _____

Write a title beside each picture below. Your title should tell what each picture is about in just a few words.

_____

_____

_____

_____

_____

_____

What's the Main Idea?

The **main idea** tells about the **whole picture**.

Does the sentence tell the main idea of the picture? Circle *yes* or *no*. Then, write the sentence that best states the main idea for each picture.

The cat wants to play.   yes   no

The cat takes a nap.   yes   no

_____

_____

The brothers play together.   yes   no

The brothers are smart.   yes   no

_____

_____

The dog is hungry.   yes   no

The dog is playful.   yes   no

_____

_____

Story Time

The **main idea** tells about the **whole story**.

Read the story below.

"Mom, can we build a fort in the dining room?" John asked.

"Sure, honey," said John's mom. Then John's mom covered the dining room table with a giant sheet. "Do you want to eat lunch in our fort?" asked John's mom.

"Yes!" said John. Then John's mom brought two peanut butter sandwiches on paper plates and sat under the table, too!

"Mom, making a fort with you is so much fun!" said John, smiling.

Does the sentence tell the main idea? Write *yes* or *no*.

1. Then John's mom covered the dining room table with a giant sheet. _____

2. "Do you want to eat lunch in our fort?" asked John's mom. _____

3. "Mom, making a fort with you is so much fun!" _____

4. Write a sentence that tells the main idea: _____

_____

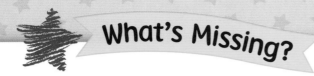

What's Missing?

Circle the object in the second picture that is different from the first picture.

Baseball Daze!

Look at the petals to find the flower that is different. Color the flower that is different.

Petal Power!

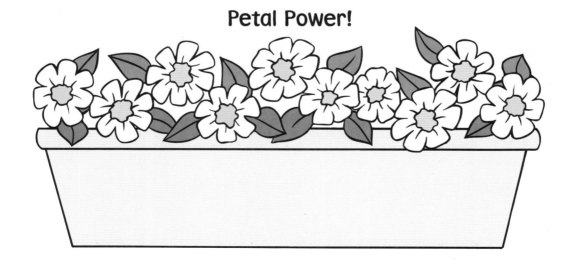

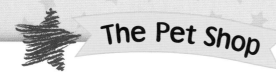

The Pet Shop

Find and circle **ten** things wrong with this picture.

Highlight Happy!

Highlighting is a strategy that will help you with your reading. When you highlight something, you use a light-colored marker to color over a special word or words that you want to remember.

Follow the directions to highlight words in the sentences below.

1. Highlight four animals you might see in Alaska.

   In Alaska, you might see bears, whales, sea otters, and moose.

2. Highlight the two things you should take to Alaska if you visit in the summer.

   If you visit Alaska in the summer, you should take bug spray and a raincoat.

3. Highlight three animals that are not from Alaska.

   Flamingos, platypuses, and lions are not from Alaska.

Sally's Snake

Name _____

Sally received a new pet snake for her birthday. Sally has a lot to learn about taking care of her new snake. She needs to know how to hold it and clean its cage. She also needs to learn what to feed it. Sally can't wait to learn how to care for her new pet!

What is the **main idea** this story? Circle your choice.

1. Sally had a great birthday.

2. Sally has a lot to learn about caring for her new pet.

3. Sally needs to learn how to hold a snake.

What is **one thing** Sally needs to learn about her new pet?

1. How to clean its cage

2. How to take pictures

3. How to read to her snake

What Is Cause and Effect?

Cause: An action or act that makes something happen.

Effect: Something that happens because of an action or cause.

Look at the following example of cause and effect.

Kyle has a spelling test and studies hard.

Kyle's hard work helps him do a super job!

Now draw a line connecting each cause on the left side of the page to its effect on the right side of the page.

More Cause and Effect!

Name _____

Cause: An action or act that makes something happen.

Effect: Something that happens because of an action or cause.

Look at the following example of cause and effect.

Now draw a line connecting each cause on the left side of the page to its effect on the right side of the page.

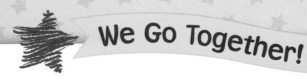

We Go Together!

Draw a line connecting the pictures that go together. Then figure out which picture is the cause and which is the effect. Write **C** for **cause** or **E** for **effect** under each picture.

_____

_____

_____

_____

_____

_____

What Happened?

Name _____

Read the stories below. Then write the missing effect.

Erin and her mom cleaned out their messy garage. Now they have room inside the garage to store Erin's bike.

Cause: Erin and her mom cleaned their messy garage.

What was the effect? _____

Frank tried out for the town basketball team and played very well. The next day, he found out that he had made the team.

Cause: Frank tried out for the town basketball team and played very well.

What was the effect? _____

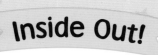

Inside Out!

Can you match the outsides with the insides? Draw a line from each picture on the left to its inside picture on the right.

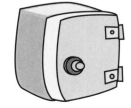

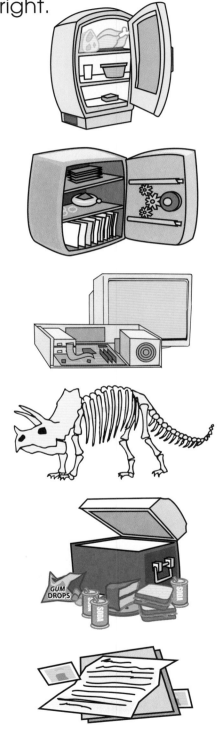

Books for Gabby!

Gabby loves to read books about many different topics. She loves to read about exotic animals. She loves stories about famous people. Gabby is also interested in becoming a doctor or an actress one day.

Look at the books below. Circle only the books that Gabby would like to read.

Famous Actresses of the Stage

How to Build a Tree House

Amazing Animals of the Amazon

Baking Muffins With Mom

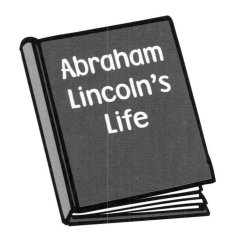

Abraham Lincoln's Life

Spend a Day With a Doctor!

CARTOON CRAZY

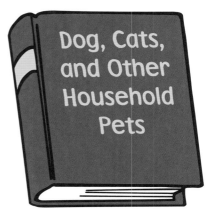

Dog, Cats, and Other Household Pets

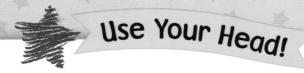

Use Your Head!

Name _____

Read each sentence below. Then read each statement that follows it. Using the information in the first sentence, decide which word best completes each statement. Then write that word on the line.

"Please put on your heavy winter coat before you go sledding," said my mom.

My mom wanted me to keep

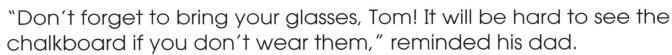

_____.   cool   warm

I put on my coat _____
I went sledding.   before   after

"Don't forget to bring your glasses, Tom! It will be hard to see the chalkboard if you don't wear them," reminded his dad.

Tom has _____ eyesight.

   good   poor

Tom is _____.

   forgetful   aware

Tom is going to _____.

   school   basketball   practice

Gifted & Talented Reading, Writing, And Math   54   Reading Comprehension
Grade 1

Where Do I Go?

Read the questions below. Then select words from the Word List to write on the lines.

Word List		
hospital	bookstore	bakery
	park	

My mom loves donuts. Dad and I wanted to surprise her with some. We stopped at the

_____.

I love to read books! My mom said she would buy me a book at the

_____.

I hurt my ankle at my basketball game. My coach took me to the

_____.

It was a warm summer day and my family went to the

_____.

Help Hattie!

Help Hattie pick out birthday presents! Read the sentences about her friends. Then write words from the Word List on the lines. Draw a picture of each present inside the boxes.

Word List

music	airplane	goggles
crayons	journal	

 Nancy loves to color pictures.

_____

 Ray wants to be a pilot.

_____

 Kristin loves to write.

_____

 Jared swims every week.

_____

 Chelsea is a great piano player.

_____

What Will Happen Next?

Name _____

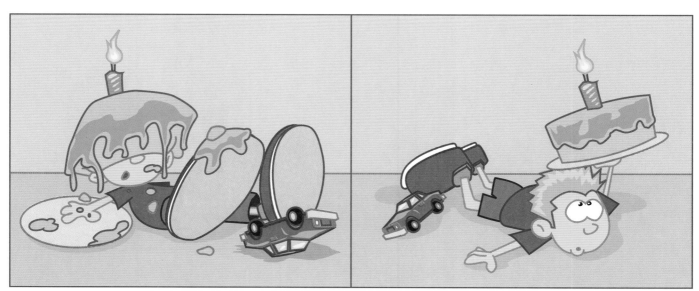

Write what happens next:

_____

_____

Name _____

What's Next?

Draw a picture of what will happen next in the boxes below:

What Happens Next?

Read each paragraph. Predict what will happen and circle your answer choice.

David and Fran go the park. The friendly ice cream man is there selling ice cream cones. "Hi kids, would you two like an ice cream cone?" he asks.

Fran and David reach into their pockets, which are empty. "We don't have any money," says Fran. The ice cream man smiles at them and reaches into his freezer. Then he says...

A) Ice cream is bad for children.

B) Today it is my treat. Free ice cream for both of you!

C) I am sorry, maybe next time.

Draw a picture of what you think will happen:

Following Directions—Animal Riddles

Fill in the letters to name an animal that fits each description. Then draw the animal in the frames.

I wish I walked faster.

__ __ __ t l e

I like to eat nuts.

__ __ __ i r r __ __

I have a very long neck.

__ __ __ __ f f e

I have black and white stripes.

__ __ __ n k

I have eight legs and spin webs.

s p __ __ __ __ __

Name _____

Finding Mistakes—Tricky Triplets

In each row, circle the two that are the same.

Stop Making Sense!

Look at the picture. A lot of silly things are happening! Draw a circle around all the things that **do** make sense.

Costume Jamboree!

Justin and his friends are dressed up for a costume party. Look at their pictures below and read the clues. Then write each child's name on the line below his or her picture. Color their costumes.

Costume clues:
- Justin and Jordan are pirates. Justin has a beard and Jordan has a mustache.
- Jackie is an animal trainer and wears pants and a neckerchief. She can make a dog jump through a hoop.
- Julie is a princess with blonde wavy hair and a bow.
- Jesse is a purple ghost and is standing next to Julie.

_____ _____ _____ _____ _____

Story Mix-Up!

Name _____

Here are some pictures from different stories. They are all mixed up.

One story is "Jack and the Beanstalk." Mark all of those pictures with a **J**. Another story is "The Three Little Pigs." Mark all of those pictures with a **P**. The third story is "Cinderella." Mark all of those pictures with a **C**.

Look at the workers below. Where would the best place be for each person to work: in the sky, on the ground, or in the water?

Put an **S** on each worker that would be in the sky. Put a **G** on each worker that would be on the ground. Put a **W** on each worker that would be in the water. Be careful! Some workers could be in more than one place.

What Can I Make?

Look at the pictures in each box below. Think about what you could make with those things. Then draw a picture of your idea.

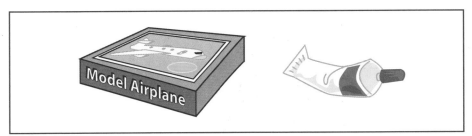

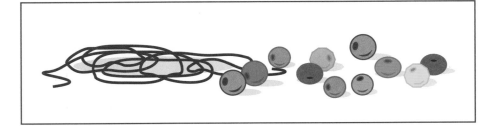

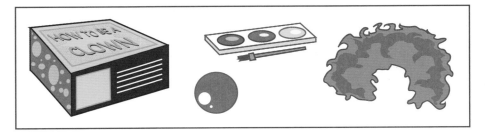

Naming Words—Nouns

A word that names a person, place, or thing is called a **noun**.

person
- girl
- cousin
- principal

place
- kitchen
- dog house
- park

thing
- ring
- cup
- baseball

Can you name these nouns?

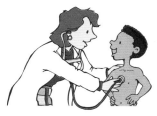 person _____

 place _____

 thing _____

Naming Words—Nouns

Name _____

Read the nouns listed below. Then write the name of each noun on your own.

duck _____

lake _____

flower _____

present _____

crocodile _____

sneakers _____

Naming Words—Nouns

Name _____

Oops! Grandpa was telling a funny story, but kept forgetting the nouns! Help Grandpa by using the nouns from the word list to fill in the blanks.

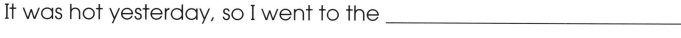

Word List

lake	flower	present
crocodile	sneakers	duck

It was hot yesterday, so I went to the _____

to swim. Suddenly, there was a green _____

with huge teeth! He got out of the water and was wearing red

_____! Then he picked a beautiful

_____ and gave it to a yellow

_____ as a _____.

I said, "I think I'm going quackers!"

The End

Action Words—Verbs

A word that tells what is happening in a sentence is called a **verb**. Verbs are **action words**.

Action Man loves verbs! Read the action words under Action Man.

dances

runs

jumps

flips

waves

In the sentences below, circle the action words.

Action Man runs.

The frog jumps.

The rabbit hops.

Action Words—Verbs

Name _____

Write an action word in each blank. Use the word list to help you.

Word List		
hops	catches	rides
shouts	swings	

Lily _____ the baseball bat!

John _____, "We scored!"

Action Man _____ on his bike.

Stacey _____ the ball.

Mom _____ the horse.

Choose two action words from Action Man that you like. Then write a sentence using each one on the lines below.

_____

_____

walks   wrestles   pitches   plays   sings   chews

Describing Words—Adjectives

A word that **describes** a noun is called an **adjective**. Adjectives tell what something is like.

Which of these two sentences is more interesting?

I bought my mom a flower.

I bought my mom a beautiful, purple, polka-dotted flower.

Read the story below or have someone read it to you. Circle the adjectives.

Mrs. Langley's tiny flower shop was special. She didn't sell regular flowers; she sold weird, wonderful, and wacky flowers. Some of her flowers were polka-dotted and others were rainbow-colored!

Draw a picture of one of Mrs. Langley's flowers.

Describing Words—Adjectives

Fill in each blank using the adjectives in the word list below.

Word List		
loud	wiggly	beautiful
kind	purple	hungry

The _____ jar was filled with grape jelly.

"Meow!" said the _____ kitten.

One hundred new _____ caterpillars are born in the spring.

The baby's rattle was so _____ no one could sleep.

The _____ old woman gave gifts to all the kids.

A _____ princess was painted by every artist in the country.

Just Me!

Look in a mirror. What do you see? Draw a picture of yourself. Then make a list of words that describe how you look, how you dress, and how you feel.

_____

_____

_____

Sentences—Complete Thoughts

A **sentence** has a **beginning** and an **ending**. A sentence tells a **complete thought**. When you write a sentence, make sure it is *all* there! Just a beginning or just an ending is not a complete sentence!

Draw a line from each sentence's beginning to its *correct* ending so that each sentence makes sense.

I ate   freckles.

Tomorrow I am going   basketball.

She plays   chocolate brownies.

He has lots of   is huge and gray.

The elephant   to the circus.

Punctuation—Periods

Use a **period** to end a **complete sentence**.
A period is like a stop sign.

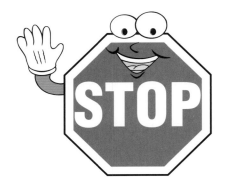

   I love to eat pizza.

   My dog barks a lot.

Mr. and Mrs. Roly-Poly went for a Sunday roll down the street. This is what they saw. Add periods at the end of each sentence.

A big dog crossed the street____

A chipmunk was digging a hole____

They saw a beautiful blue jay____

Mrs. Roly-Poly saw a baby bunny____

Someone dropped a quarter____

Punctuation—Question Marks

A **question** is a sentence that **asks** something.
Its first word begins with a capital letter.
A question ends with a question mark (?).

Why did the man throw the clock out the window?
(To see time fly!)

Trace these question marks. Then write some of your
own. Circle your two most awesome question marks!

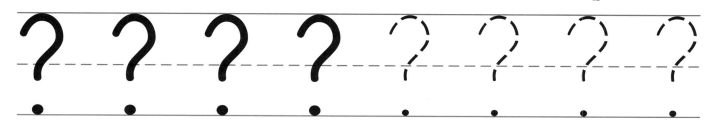

Below are some more riddles for you. Add a question mark at the
end of each sentence that asks something.

Why is it so hot after a ball game____   (Because all the fans leave!)

Why did the cookie go to the hospital____   (Because he felt crummy!)

What insect gets an A in English____   (A spelling bee!)

What goes up and never comes down____   (Your age!)

Capital Letters Rule!

1. The **first word** of a sentence always begins with a capital letter.
   The fat bear is very hungry.

2. **People's names** always begin with a capital letter.
   Todd and I like to eat cupcakes.

3. The name of a **place** always begins with a capital letter.
   It is very hot and sunny in California.

4. The names of **months** always begin with a capital letter.
   My birthday is in June.

5. The **days** of the week always begin with a capital letter.
   We had a wacky day at my school on Wednesday.

6. The days of **holidays** always begin with a capital letter.
   Many people eat turkey on Thanksgiving.

June

Sunday	Monday	Tuesday	Wednesday	Thursday	Friday	Saturday
						1
2	3	4	5	6	7	8
9	10	11	12	13	14	15
16	17	18	19	20	21	22
23	24	25	26	27	28	29
30						

Capital Letters Rule!

Read the sentences below and circle the words that need a capital letter. Then write each sentence correctly.

on tuesday we go to computer class.

_____

the fourth of july is my favorite holiday.

_____

in the summer, hawaii is very hot.

_____

my brother's birthday is august 21st.

_____

sara and gabriel are twins.

_____

i think blueberry pancakes are yummy.

_____

Sentence Starters

Name _____

Write an ending for each of these sentences.

The zebra _____

_____

My sister Zelda _____

_____

The magic book _____

_____

There was a strange _____

_____

The table broke because _____

_____

Sentence Starters

Write an ending for each of these sentences.

A bumblebee landed _____

_____

The balloon flew _____

_____

My dog yawned _____

_____

When I woke up _____

_____

Tiger's new glasses _____

_____

Sentence Endings

Write a beginning for each of these sentences.

_____

_____ under my bed!

_____

_____ everyone cheered for me!

_____

_____ a mouse was in my sock!

_____

_____ in the ocean.

_____

_____ on the roof.

Sentence Endings

Write a beginning for each of these sentences.

_____

_____ from a rocket ship.

_____

_____ in the dark.

_____

_____ in my soup!

_____

_____ on my head!

_____

_____ tasted like crunchy bugs!

Sequencing

Carefully tear out page 85. Cut out the square pictures. Match the pictures with the correct sentences. Then glue the pictures to this page.

I think I'll make a snowman.

It's getting taller!

Now he'll need a head.

A scarf will keep him warm.

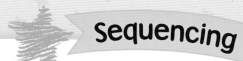

Sequencing

Name _____

Tear out this page. Cut the pictures apart. Put them in order and then glue them onto page 84.

This page is left blank for the
cutting activity on the other side.

Name _____

Beginning, Middle, and End

All stories have three parts:

Beginning

Our bags were packed.

Middle

We crossed the desert.

End

We found the buried treasure!

The three sentences below are out of order! Write the sentences in order (beginning, middle, and end) to make a story.

There was lots of snow!

My cousin, Nanuk, invited me to the Arctic.

We built a huge igloo.

_____

_____

_____

Beginning, Middle, and End

All stories have a beginning, a middle, and an end. Below are three sentences out of order! Write the sentences in order to make a story. Then draw a picture of the story.

Underwater we saw a giant fish.

I went snorkeling with my friend.

We put on flippers and goggles.

_____

_____

_____

Order Words

Order words tell what happens **first**, **next**, and **last**.

First, we got on the ship.

Next, we sailed across the ocean.

Last, we arrived at the tropical island!

Label the pictures below to show what happened **first**, **next**, and **last**.

_____

_____

_____

_____

_____

_____

Name _____

Read the story below and circle the **order words** you learned on the previous page.

I have waited all year for my birthday! First, I hang colorful streamers. Next, I help blow up balloons and put candy in little bags on the table. Last, I open the door and welcome my friends to my party!

 **Using Order Words**

Draw a picture about your birthday. Then write how you get ready for your birthday party. Be sure to use the order words **first**, **next**, and **last** in your writing.

_____

_____

_____

_____

Endings

Name _____

The next few stories have beginnings and middles, but no endings! They need YOU to complete the stories by writing an ending for each one. Use your imagination and what you read in the story to write an ending. Don't forget to read the stories aloud after you're finished.

African Safari!

"Keep your head in the jeep!" shouted the driver as we raced along the plains of Africa. A ferocious lion that we accidentally woke from a nap was chasing our jeep! Suddenly, the jeep made a funny noise. The driver said, "Folks, we seem to have a little problem…"

_____

_____

_____

_____

_____

Endings

Name _____

Finish the story below.

Kids in Space!

"Ten, nine, eight…oh my gosh!…seven, six, five…I can't believe it! … four…three… I will be the first kid in the entire world to travel in space…two…one…BLAST OFF!" The space shuttle powered up through the sky traveling deep into outer space. I looked out the space shuttle window and saw…

_____

_____

_____

_____

Beginnings and Middles

This story has an ending, but it doesn't have a beginning or middle! Read the ending, and then write a beginning, and middle. After you are finished, read your story aloud.

The Rickety Roller-Coaster!

_____

_____

_____

_____

_____

"Wow, that was some ride! I don't know if I'll ever ride a roller coaster again!" I said.

"Are you kidding?" Scott replied. "That was the most fun I've ever had! Come on, let's do it again!"

The End

Beginnings and Middles

This story has an ending, but it doesn't have a beginning or middle! Read the ending, and then write a beginning and middle for it.

Gilbert, the Tap-Dancing Horse!

_____

_____

_____

_____

Gilbert's picture was in all of the papers! *The Tap-Dancing Horse Is the Star of Broadway!* read the newspaper headlines. "Well, Gilbert, you're a star! It was a good idea to send you to tap-dancing school after all," said Mr. Peters. Then Gilbert put on a special show for the entire farm.

The End

Name _____

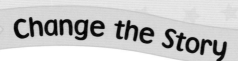
Change the Story

Sometimes it is fun to change a story, especially a story everybody knows. Read the story below.

Snow White

Once upon a time there was a beautiful princess named Snow White. For many days she walked in the woods until she came to a tiny house. Suddenly, the door opened and out popped seven dwarfs with the strangest names!

Now write the story again, changing the words in red. Use your imagination. Give the story a new title. Then read your story aloud to hear what you've written.

_____

_____

_____

_____

_____

_____

_____

Change the Story

Name _____

Sometimes it is fun to change a story, especially a story everybody knows. Read the story below.

Pinocchio

Once upon a time there was a wooden puppet who was made of magic wood. His name was Pinocchio, and he could talk! More than anything, he wished he were a real boy...

Now write the story again, changing the words in red. Use your imagination. Give the story a new title. Then read your story aloud to hear what you've written.

_____

_____

_____

_____

_____

_____

_____

Follow the Pictures

Here is a story told only in pictures. Follow the pictures and write the story below.

_____

_____

_____

_____

_____

_____

_____

_____

_____

_____

_____

_____

Follow the Pictures

Here is a story told only in pictures. Follow the pictures and write the story below.

_____

_____

_____

_____

_____

_____

_____

_____

_____

_____

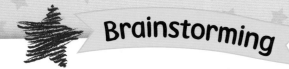

Brainstorming

Brainstorming means thinking of everything you can about a topic. Think of a giant storm of ideas coming into your head!

In the "idea clouds" below, write down all the ideas you can think of for the topic, "The First Day of School." Remember, there are no right or wrong words, or good or bad ideas. Just write whatever comes into your brain. Some ideas are already filled in for you.

The First Day of School

Narrowing Your Idea

Look at your "idea clouds" about the first day of school from the previous page. Pick a few of your new ideas to write a story.

The First Day of School

_____

_____

_____

_____

_____

_____

_____

_____

_____

_____

_____

_____

_____

_____

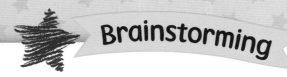

Brainstorming

Circle one of the ideas from the list below. Then write down words about that idea.

Idea List

| Animals at the zoo | My teacher | New sneakers |
| Summer vacation | Basketball | A secret wish |

_____

_____

_____

_____

_____

_____

_____

_____

_____

_____

Narrowing Your Idea

Look at your idea list on the previous page. Use your list to help you write a story about the topic you chose.

_____

_____

_____

_____

_____

_____

_____

_____

_____

_____

_____

_____

_____

Story Beginnings

Name _____

This story has a middle and an ending, but it doesn't have a beginning! Write a beginning for this story.

The Amazon Adventure!

_____

_____

_____

_____

_____

_____

"…and I am Suka Chakalocka. We are having a feast in your honor for bringing the medicine to our village."

"What fun!" I said, and joined in the feast.

The next day, my plane came back to pick me up. Suka Chakalocka said, "Thank you, brave one. You are welcome in the Amazon anytime!"

The End

Story Beginnings

The next story has a middle and an ending, but it doesn't have a beginning! Write a beginning for this story.

Candy Town Sleepover!

_____

_____

_____

_____

_____

_____

    Then Noah showed me his room. I could hardly believe my eyes. His bed was a cupcake and his pillows were marshmallows! Candy canes hung in his closet! I had never seen so much candy in my whole life! I sat down to rest on his gumdrop chair. I hoped I would be invited to sleep over at Noah's again!

The End

Story Middles

This story has a beginning and an ending, but it is missing its middle! Use your imagination and what you read in the story to write a middle on the lines below. Don't forget to read the story aloud after you're finished.

A Whale of a Birthday!

I opened my birthday present excitedly. Inside was a coupon from my Aunt Carol. It read, "Good for one family whale-watching adventure. Please wear warm clothes!" Wow! A real whale-watching adventure…

_____

_____

_____

_____

_____

_____

"This was the best birthday present I ever had!" I said, "and we didn't need warm clothes—we needed *bathing suits*! It really was a *whale* of a party!"

The End

Story Middles

Name _____

This story has a beginning and an ending, but it is missing its middle! Write a middle for the story on the lines below.

Tick Tock Todd!

"Don't eat that pie! Don't eat that pie!" screamed the cook as he ran out of the kitchen into the restaurant. Todd had just swallowed the last piece of cherry pie. "My watch fell into the batter and was baked into the pie by accident," cried the chef. Suddenly, Todd started ticking…

_____

_____

_____

_____

Todd said to the reporter, "Yes, cherry pie is still my favorite pie, but I will miss being a human clock! Although, I do think it's *time* things got back to normal!"

The End

Story Endings

Name _____

This story has a beginning and a middle, but no ending! See if you can complete the story by writing an ending below.

Sleeping Shoes!

Things were definitely strange when I slept over at my cousin Rachel's house. "What are you doing?" I asked Rachel, who was putting her shoes to bed in a birdcage!

"I'm putting my shoes to bed, of course," she replied. "If I don't put them in a cage, they will walk off at night." Then she went to sleep.

In the middle of the night, I tiptoed to her shoe cage and undid the lock…

_____

_____

_____

_____

_____

_____

Story Endings

This story has a beginning and a middle, but no ending! Write an ending for the story below.

Bubble Gum Inventions!

One day, Elaine came home from school and said, "I am not riding the bus to school anymore. I am going to fly to school from now on!"

Soon her family heard banging sounds coming from the basement! Pink bubbles were coming from under the basement door...

_____

_____

_____

_____

_____

_____

_____

_____

Bringing It All Together

What if you woke up one morning and the inside of your house was upside down? That would mean your bed would be stuck to the ceiling! Instead of walking on the floor, you would be walking on the ceiling! Would you call for help? Would you crawl back into bed? Would you dance on the ceiling? Write (brainstorm!) your ideas on the lines below to get ready to write your own story!

Upside-Down Morning!

_____

_____

_____

_____

_____

_____

_____

_____

Bringing It All Together

Use your ideas on the previous page to write your own story. Remember, a great story has an exciting beginning, middle, and ending. Good luck!

Upside-Down Morning!

By _____

_____

_____

_____

_____

_____

_____

_____

_____

_____

_____

_____

Making It Better—Describing Words

Remember your adjectives! **Adjectives** are **describing words** that tell us more about something. They make our writing more interesting.

Adjectives tell:

What Kind: ugly shirt   red hat   new bike

How Many: five kittens   several presents

Which One: that desk   this room   those crayons

Complete each sentence below by writing a describing word (adjective) in the blank. Use the word list to help you.

Word List		
gigantic	sticky	soft
scary	noisy	yellow
seven	lumpy	

1. The _____ bed was fun to jump on!

2. _____ chairs were stuck to the ceiling when I woke up!

3. I was afraid I would fall out of my _____ bed and land on the floor!

Making It Better—Describing Words

Remember: **Adjectives** are describing words that tell **what kind, how many** or **how much**, and **which one**.

Look at each picture and write a word that describes it.

 _____

 _____

 _____

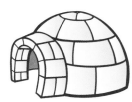 _____

 _____

 _____

 _____

 _____

Proofreading—Punctuation

Now that you're writing your own stories, it is time for a little proofreading! **Proofreading** helps you fix mistakes in **spelling**, **punctuation**, and **capitalization**.

First, meet Professor Proofhead!

Professor Proofhead would like to show you some exciting proofreading marks.

⬭ misspelling

≡ make a capital letter

⊙ add a period

? add a question mark

! add an exclamation mark

See how Professor Proofhead uses the proofreading marks below.

I love my (dogg). My dog is (verryy) smart and likes to come to school with me⊙ <u>w</u>hy does my dog like school so much? <u>m</u>y dog loves school because he is a watch dog and can tell time better than most kids in my (classs) ⊙ <u>m</u>y dog is the best dog in the (werld) !

Proofreading—Punctuation

It is time to practice proofreading. Remember, you are looking for mistakes in:

Spelling: My (dogg) is silly.

Punctuation: Wow! You are so funny.

Capitalization: mr. smith tells funny jokes.

Professor Proofhead is here to help you!

Proofread the following sentences:

   I love too swim. i love to swim moore than most fissh Swimming is my favorite sport because i am super goode at it I kan swim fast. i like to swim in mi pool, but once i swam in the ocean wit my dad

Proofread these sentences, too:

tuesday is pizza day at my school

do you want to come too mi partee

mr north is taking us to the circus on fridae

Final Draft—With Illustration!

Remember, using correct punctuation and spelling makes your story easier to read. Adding describing words helps your reader enjoy your story more.

Now you are ready to write the final draft of "Upside-Down Morning!" (see page 111). Don't forget to include an illustration! After you are finished, read your story aloud.

_____

_____

_____

_____

_____

_____

_____

_____

_____

_____

_____

_____

_____

_____

_____

_____

_____

Three Things You Like About Your Story!

On the lines below, write three things that you like best about your story. Ask yourself: Is my story original? Is it creative? Is it funny? Is it scary? Is my story filled with mistakes, or is it easy to read?

Favorite (number one! totally awesome!) thing about my story:

_____

_____

_____

_____

Second favorite thing about my story:

_____

_____

_____

_____

Third favorite thing about my story:

_____

_____

_____

_____

Name _____

Three Things Someone Else Likes About Your Story!

Have someone read your final draft of "Upside-Down Morning!" (see page 116). Then ask him or her to write down three favorite things that he or she liked best about your work.

Favorite thing about "Upside-Down Morning!" by

_____ was:

_____

_____

_____

Second favorite thing about the story was:

_____

_____

_____

Third favorite thing about the story was:

_____

_____

_____

Write a Friendly Letter

Friendly letters are fun to write. It's nice to send letters to friends and relatives. It's also nice to receive letters, too! There are rules for writing certain types of letters. Every type of letter is made of these parts.

> The **date** must go at the top, right-hand side of the letter.

> The letter begins with a **greeting**, usually *Dear*, and the name of the person. Always put a comma after the person's name.

June 15, 2002

Dear Kristin,

   I can't wait to tell you about a story I wrote. It is fantastic!

It is about a girl who travels to the Amazon jungle and meets

an Amazon guide named Suka Chakalocka! Suka invites the

girl to a jungle feast! I hope you like reading my story!

Sincerely,

Allison

> The main part of a letter is called the **body**.

> The letter ends with a **closing**. You can write *Sincerely*, or *Yours truly*. The first word in the closing is always capitalized. Always put a comma after the closing.

> The writer signs his or her name at the bottom. This is called the **signature**.

Write a Letter Describing Your Story

Look back at your "Upside-Down Morning!" story. Write a letter to a friend or relative telling him or her about your story. Some parts of the letter are filled in to help you get started.

_____
(date)

Dear_____,
　　(greeting)

_____

_____

_____

_____

_____

_____
(body)

Sincerely,
(closing)

_____
(signature)

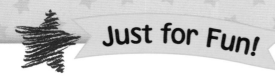

Just for Fun!

Write a story using all five words listed below. After you are finished, read your story aloud and don't forget to give it a title. Have fun!

Funny Words		
feather	jam	stick
wig	gumballs	

_____ (title)

_____

_____

_____

_____

_____

_____

_____

_____

Write a story using one of the ideas below. Then draw a picture to go with your story.

Idea List

My dog thinks he is a bird

My real name is...

My favorite color

The day my hair turned purple

_____

_____

_____

_____

Just for Fun!

Name _____

Write a story using all five words listed below. After you are finished, read your story aloud and don't forget to give it a title. Have fun!

Funny Words		
polka dots	stripes	bubbly water
fairy	wishes	

_____ (title)

By _____

_____

_____

_____

_____

_____

_____

_____

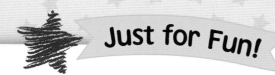

Write a story using one of the ideas below. Then draw a picture to go with your story.

Idea List

I looked out my window and saw…

I lost my…

I found a magic shell

My dog loves to watch T.V.

_____

_____

_____

_____

_____

Spilled Numbers

Derek dropped his box of numbered cards.
The cards are numbered from 1 to 20.

Look at the numbers carefully. There are three cards still left in the box.

Which numbers are they? _____

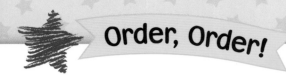

Name _____

Order, Order!

The mice in each row are to line up in order according to their numbers, from smallest to largest. But some mice are not in the right place. In each row, circle the mouse that is out of order. Draw an arrow to show where that mouse should go.

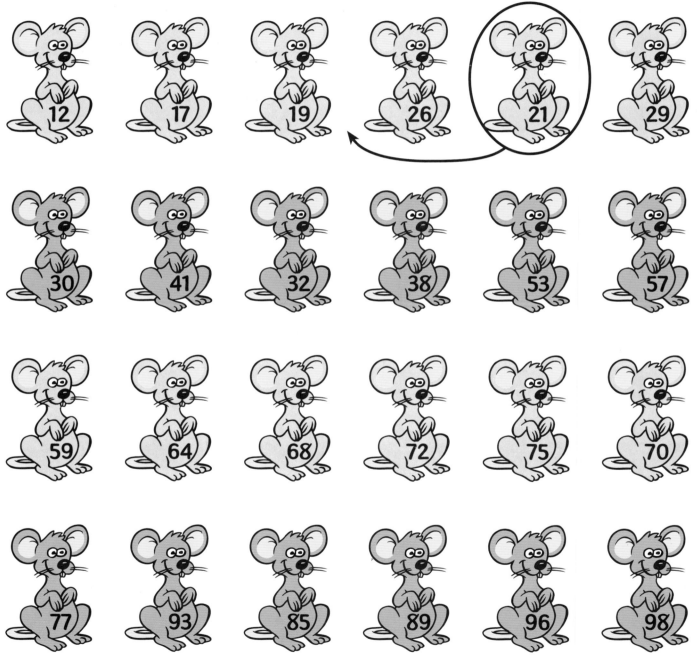

Row 1: 12 17 19 26 (21) 29

Row 2: 30 41 32 38 53 57

Row 3: 59 64 68 72 75 70

Row 4: 77 93 85 89 96 98

On the Road

These cars are supposed to be traveling in order, from the largest to the smallest number. But some cars are not in the right place. In each row, circle the car that is out of order. Draw an arrow to show where that car should go.

Who's Who?

Name _____

Use the clues to help you write the correct names on the lines.

1. I am younger than all of the girls. I am not the youngest.

   Who am I? _____

2. I am older than Eric. I am younger than Becky.

   Who am I? _____

3. I am older than two of the girls. I am not a boy.

   Who am I? _____

4. I am not a girl. I am older than Abby.

   Who am I? _____

5. I am a boy. I am five years younger than the oldest boy.

   Who am I? _____

6. I am younger than Abby. I am older than Joni.

   Who am I? _____

Mouse and Cheese

An even number ends in 2, 4, 6, 8, or 0. Look at the numbers below. Help the mouse get to the cheese by coloring a path of even numbers.

12	24	6	3
7	11	5	14	21
18	26	10	2	15
4	13	1	19	17
8	22	16	20	

Write the even numbers on the path in order from smallest to largest.

_____

_____

Flying Home

An odd number ends in 1, 3, 5, 7, or 9. Help the bee get to its home by coloring a path of odd numbered flowers.

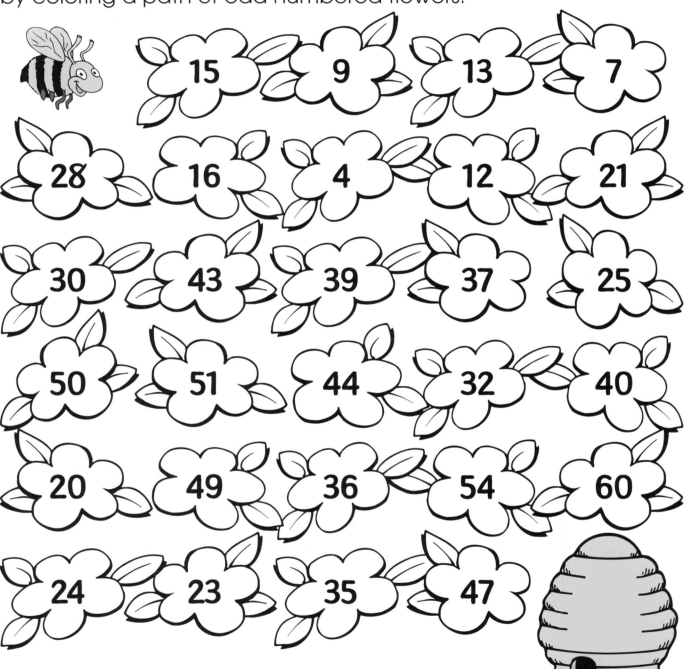

Which number on the path is the largest odd number? _____

Cooking Up Numbers

Look at the numbers in the bowls below. Use them to write numbers that match the clues. For each set of clues, do not use a number in a bowl more than once.

1. The number is even. It is greater than 30. It is less than 35.

_____

2. The number is odd. It is greater than 50. It is less than 60.

_____

5. The number is even. It is greater than 70. It is less than 90.

_____

3. The number is even. It is greater than 60. It is less than 70.

_____

6. The number is odd. It is greater than 75. It is less than 85.

_____

4. The number is odd. It is greater than 25. It is less than 40.

_____

7. The number is even. It is greater than 80. It is less than 90.

_____

Mystery Numbers

Name _____

Read each set of clues. Figure out the mystery numbers. Then write them on the lines.

1.
> The number is odd.
>
> The number is more than 9.
>
> The number is less than 13.
>
> The mystery number is _____.

2.
> The number is even.
>
> The number is more than 8 + 8.
>
> The number is less than 10 + 10.
>
> The mystery number is _____.

3. The number is more than 50.

The number is less than 70.

Count by tens, and you say the number.

The mystery number is _____.

4. The number is more than 30.

The number is less than 40.

Count by fives, and you say the number.

The mystery number is _____.

Make up your own clues for a mystery number.
Ask a friend or family member to figure out the mystery number.

_____

_____

_____

What's in the Hat?

Name _____

Michael the Magician has a great trick. He pulls bunnies out of his hat! Read each clue. Count the bunnies you see. Then write how many bunnies are hiding in Michael's hat.

1. There are 7 bunnies in all.

How many are in the hat? _____

4. There are 9 bunnies in all.

How many are in the hat? _____

2. There are 10 bunnies in all.

How many are in the hat? _____

5. There are 14 bunnies in all.

How many are in the hat? _____

3. There are 12 bunnies in all.

How many are in the hat? _____

6. There are 15 bunnies in all.

How many are in the hat? _____

Make Them Equal

Name _____

Look at the numbers in each row. Write **+** or **–** in the circles to make two number sentences that are equal.

1. 6 (**+**) 3 = 11 (**-**) 2

2. 5 ( ) 2 = 10 ( ) 7

3. 6 ( ) 2 = 12 ( ) 4

4. 8 ( ) 6 = 9 ( ) 5

5. 12 ( ) 3 = 17 ( ) 8

6. 16 ( ) 8 = 5 ( ) 3

7. 9 ( ) 6 = 8 ( ) 7

8. 11 ( ) 3 = 17 ( ) 9

Find and Circle

Look at the numbers in the box. Circle three numbers that add up to 10. The numbers can go across or down. Keep going until you have found all the sets. When you are done, all the numbers in the box should be circled.

3	2	6	1	3
2	8	5	4	1
5	0	9	0	1
4	4	2	2	2
7	3	0	2	7
1	8	1	6	1

Sums to 12

Use the numbers 1 to 9. Find three different numbers that add up to 12. Write them in the boxes below. See if you can make four number sentences. (You cannot use a number more than once in each sentence.)

☐ + ☐ + ☐ = **12**

☐ + ☐ + ☐ = **12**

☐ + ☐ + ☐ = **12**

☐ + ☐ + ☐ = **12**

Now write number sentences with four numbers that add up to 12.

☐ + ☐ + ☐ + ☐ = **12**

☐ + ☐ + ☐ + ☐ = **12**

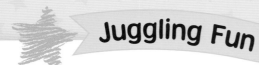

Juggling Fun

Name _____

Write the numbers 1 to 9 on the juggling balls. Use each number only once. The sum of the three numbers on each cat's juggling balls must match the number on that cat's tag.

High-Flying Numbers

Write the numbers 1 to 9 in the three sections of the hot-air balloons. The three numbers on each balloon must add up to 15. Use each number only once. Cross off the numbers on the cloud as you use them. Three of the numbers have been filled in for you.

Party Time

Solve these problems.

1. There are 8 children at a birthday party. There is the same number of boys and girls.

   How many children are boys?

   _____

   How many children are girls? _____

2. There are 12 balloons. For every red balloon, there are 2 yellow balloons.

   How many balloons are red? _____

   How many balloons are yellow?

   _____

3. There are 8 presents at the party. Some presents are in boxes and some are in bags. There are 4 more boxes than bags.

   How many boxes are there? _____

   How many bags are there? _____

Frankie Frog

Frankie Frog loves to jump! He also loves to jump and make patterns. Look at the number lines below. Figure out the patterns. For each pattern, write the next number that Frankie will land on.

1.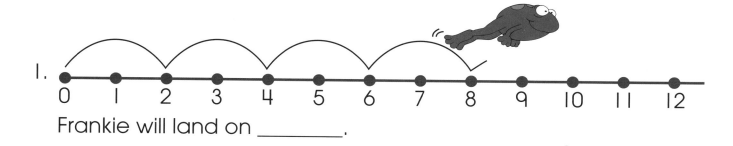

Frankie will land on _____.

2.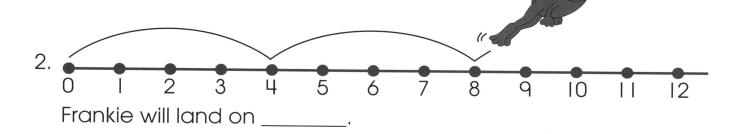

Frankie will land on _____.

3.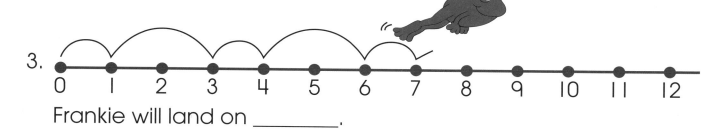

Frankie will land on _____.

4.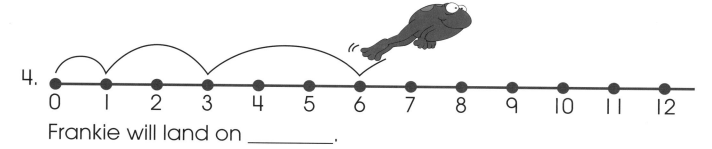

Frankie will land on _____.

All Aboard!

Figure out the pattern on each train. Then fill in the missing numbers.

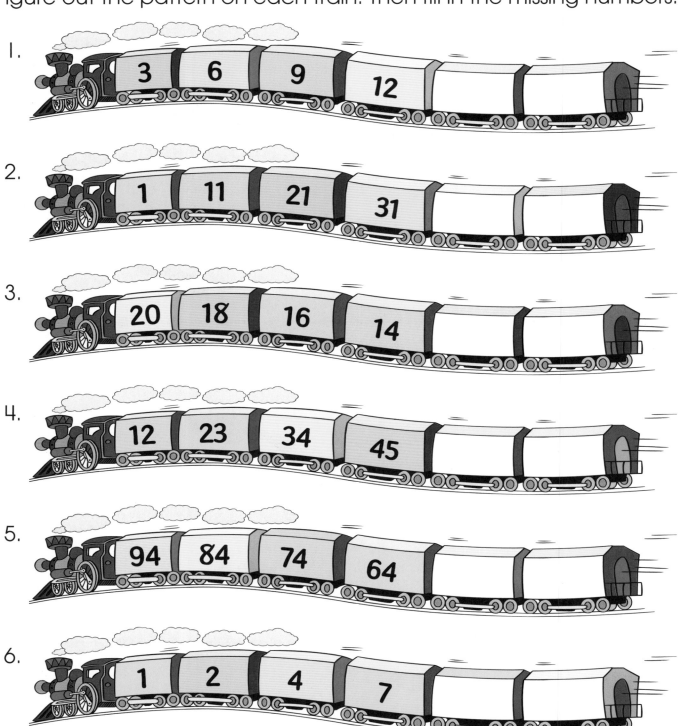

1. 3 6 9 12

2. 1 11 21 31

3. 20 18 16 14

4. 12 23 34 45

5. 94 84 74 64

6. 1 2 4 7

Caterpillar Patterns

Study the pattern on each caterpillar. Then complete the pattern.

1.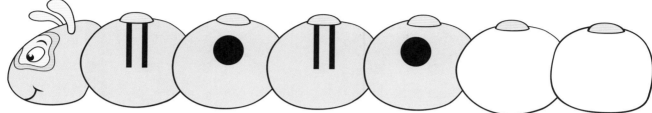

2.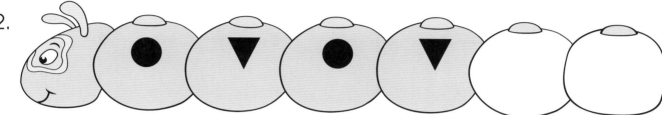

3.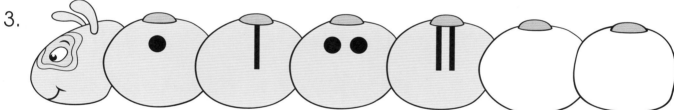

4.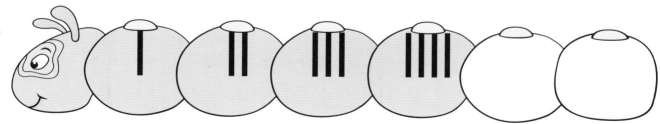

5.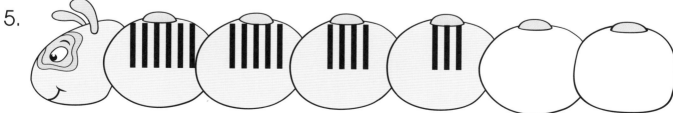

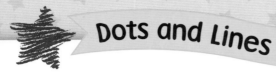
Dots and Lines

Name _____

Connect the dots to extend each pattern.

1.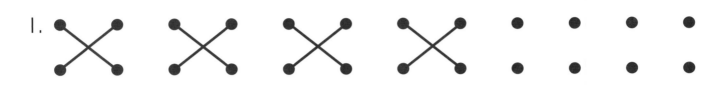

2.

3.

4.

5.

Now connect the dots to make your own pattern!

Shape Patterns

Look at each row. Draw the shape that comes next.

1. 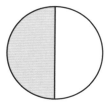   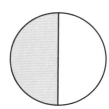

2. 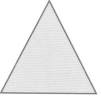   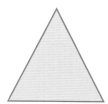

3.   

4. 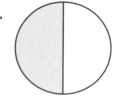   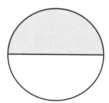   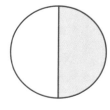

5.    

6.       

Piggy Bank Riddles

Read the clues. Draw what is in each piggy bank. Show quarters, nickels, dimes, and pennies.

1. There are two coins.
   They add up to 35¢.

2. There are three coins.
   They add up to 20¢.

3. There are three coins.
   They add up to 45¢.

4. There are four coins.
   They add up to 50¢.

5. There are five coins.
   They add up to 46¢.

Make 25 Cents

Draw coins to show eight different ways you can make 25 cents.

1.	5.
2.	6.
3.	7.
4.	8.

Coin Patterns

Name _____

Solve these problems involving patterns with coins.

1. Jack had some coins. He began laying them out in a pattern like this:

Jack used ten coins. How many cents did he have? Label the coins below, and write the amount to show your answer.

= _____ ¢

2. Lisa laid out some coins in a pattern, too. Her pattern looked like this:

How much money did Lisa have after she laid down ten coins? Label the coins below, and write the amount to show your answer.

= _____ ¢

3. Who had more money—Jack or Lisa? _____

A Toy Sale

This sale sign was posted at a toy shop. Look at the prices of the toys. Then solve the problems.

Super Sale!		
Whistle	—	5 cents
Top	—	10 cents
Car	—	15 cents
Yo-yo	—	20 cents

1. Amanda bought two different toys. She spent 20 cents. What did she buy? _____

2. Jessie bought three different toys. He spent 35 cents. What did he buy? _____

3. Carl and Lee each bought a toy. Carl's toy cost 15 cents more than Lee's toy. What did each child buy? Carl _____ Lee _____

4. Janet wants to spend exactly 25 cents. List the different sets of toys she could buy.

_____

_____

_____

_____

Some children went to the balloon shop. Write the letters of the balloons they bought.

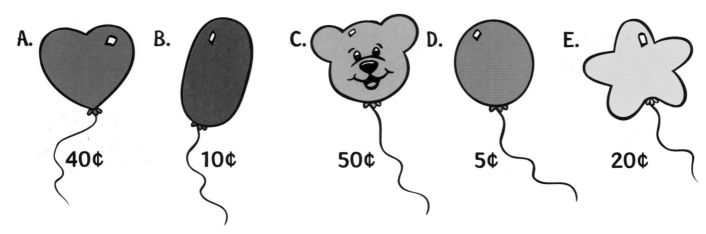

A. 40¢   B. 10¢   C. 50¢   D. 5¢   E. 20¢

1. Sam bought two balloons. He paid 30 cents. Which balloons did he buy? _____

2. Shannon bought two balloons. She paid 70 cents. Which balloons did she buy? _____

3. Mark wanted to buy two different balloons. What is the least amount of money he could have spent? _____ What is the most amount of money he could have spent?

    _____

4. Katie bought three different balloons. She spent 80 cents. Which balloons did she buy? _____

5. Kent bought three different balloons. He spent 65 cents. Which balloons did he buy? _____

A Flower Garden

Mrs. Potter has eight flowers in her garden. Each flower is a solid color. The flowers are red, purple, orange, or yellow.

Read the clues. Figure out how many flowers of each color Mrs. Potter has. Then color the flowers.

Clues:
- There are more yellow flowers than orange flowers.

- There are more red flowers than purple flowers.

- There are the same number of yellow and purple flowers.

Toy Bunnies

Name _____

Megan has six toy bunnies. Each one is a different color. Megan also has three baskets. She will put two bunnies in each basket.

Read the clues. Then color the pictures to show how Megan will pair the bunnies.

Clues: • The pink bunny can go with the black bunny or the blue bunny.

• The brown bunny can go with the purple bunny or the black bunny.

• The purple bunny can go only with the yellow bunny.

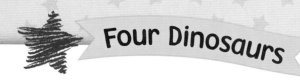

Four Dinosaurs

Name _____

There are four dinosaurs standing in a line. Read the clues below. Then color the dinosaurs to show in which order they are standing.

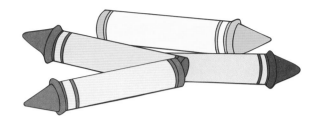

Clues: • The green dinosaur is behind the yellow dinosaur.

• The brown dinosaur is behind the red dinosaur.

• The brown dinosaur is not the last in line.

Four Brothers

Ted, Ed, Fred, and Jed are brothers. Use the clues to find out which boy is the shortest, which boy is the tallest, and which boys are in-between. Then write their names under their pictures.

Clues: • Ed is taller than Fred.

• Ted is taller than Jed.

• Fred is taller than Ted.

_____   _____   _____   _____

Taking a Trip

The Lang family is going on a trip. Read the clues to find out where the family members sit in the van. Then write their names on the correct seat.

Clues: • One parent drives.

• Matt, the youngest, sits behind his mom.

• Ruff, the family's dog, sits in the back.

• Anna sits behind the driver.

• Eric sits behind his little brother.

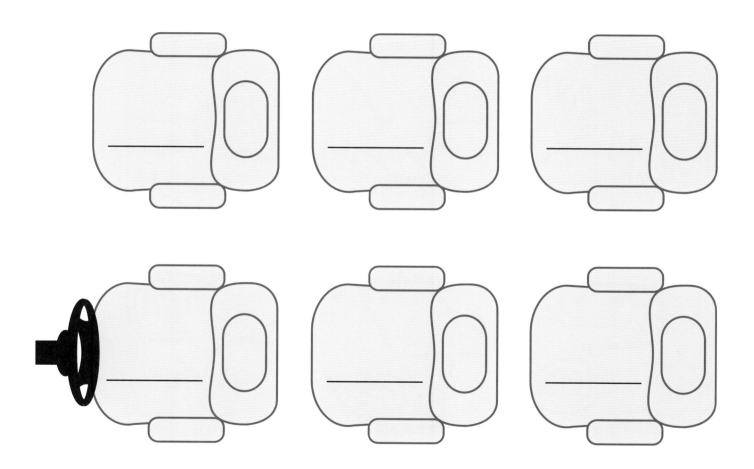

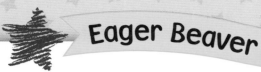

Eager Beaver

Name _____

Eager Beaver has gathered a pile of sticks to begin building his lodge. Now he has changed his mind, and he wants to move his lodge somewhere else! Eager Beaver must move one stick at a time. He cannot move any stick that is covered by another stick. Look at the picture below. Number the sticks from 1 to 6 to show the order Eager Beaver must move them.

Sorting Shapes

Miss Baker asked her class to sort eight shapes into two groups. Look at how Randy and Sandy sorted the shapes. Then label each group.

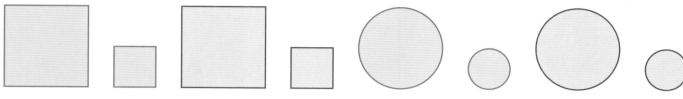

Randy's Groups

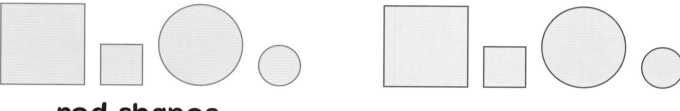

red shapes _____   _____

Sandy's Groups

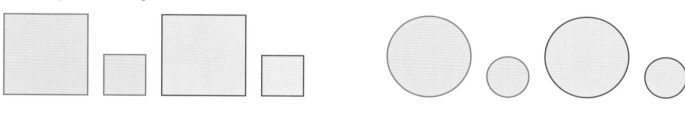

_____   _____

Draw two other groups you could make with the shapes. Label your groups.

_____   _____

Circus Fun

Name _____

Here comes the circus parade! Read these problems and solve them.

1. Kristen was watching the clowns and horses in the parade. She counted 7 heads and 20 legs. How many clowns and horses did she see?

   clowns _____ horses _____

2. Some clowns in the parade were riding bicycles. Other clowns were riding tricycles. There were 12 wheels in all. How many bicycles and tricycles were there?

   bicycles _____ tricycles _____

3. One clown was holding red and blue balloons. The clown had 15 balloons altogether. There were twice as many red balloons as there were blue balloons. How many balloons were red and how many were blue?

   red balloons _____ blue balloons _____

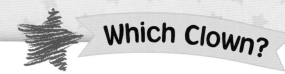
Which Clown?

Read each set of clues. Write the letter of the clown that is being described.

A   B   C   D   E

1. He has a hat.
   He has suspenders.
   He has dots.

   _____

3. He has no hat.
   He has dots.
   He has no necktie.

   _____

2. He has suspenders.
   He has no hat.
   He has a necktie.

   _____

4. He has no necktie.
   He has stripes.
   He has a hat.

   _____

Which clown is not described above? _____ Write three clues about him.

_____

_____

_____

Roger's Triangles

Name _____

Roger has made some special triangles. Study the numbers on the triangles carefully. Then fill in the missing numbers.

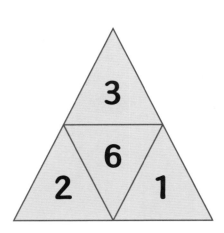

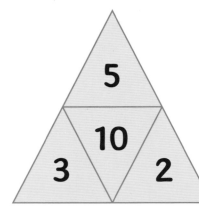

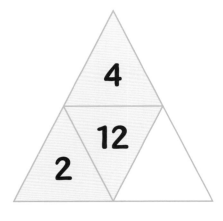

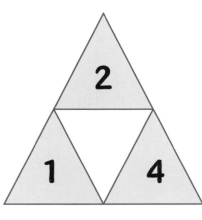

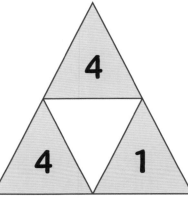

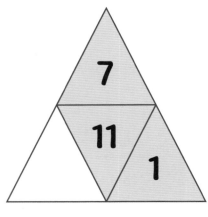

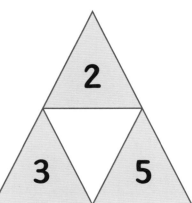

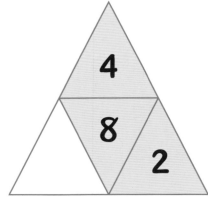

How Many Cookies?

Name _____

Mrs. Lee made some cookies for her friends. She put the cookies in round boxes and square boxes. All the round boxes had the same number of cookies. All the square boxes had the same number of cookies.

Study the pictures. Figure out how many cookies were in each box.

 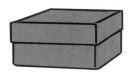 = 16 cookies

  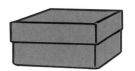 = 22 cookies

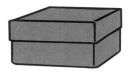 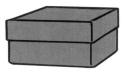  = 26 cookies

How many cookies were in the  ? _____

How many cookies were in the 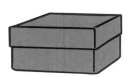 ? _____

Library Lineup

Eight children are waiting for the library to open. Look at the lineup and solve the problems.

1. Sue is fifth in line. How many children are behind Sue? _____

2. Matt is third in line. How many children are behind Matt? _____

3. Eric is sixth in line. How many children are before him? _____

4. Jill is fourth in line. Amy is eighth in line. How many children are between Jill and Amy? _____

5. Lee is second in line. Toby is seventh in line. How many children are between Lee and Toby? _____

6. Dan is first in line. How many children are between him and the last boy in line? _____

7. Write the names of the children in the order they are lined up. Begin with the first child and end with the last.

_____

_____

To the Doghouse

Guess the length of each path in inches. Write your guess in the box labeled **My Guess**. Then check your guess by measuring the path with a ruler. Write the actual length in the box labeled **My Check**.

———
one inch

1.

My Guess	My Check

2.

My Guess	My Check

3.

My Guess	My Check

4.

My Guess	My Check

Paper Caterpillars

Name _____

Mr. Parker's class glued paper circles together to make caterpillars. Solve the following problems to find out how long some of the caterpillars were.

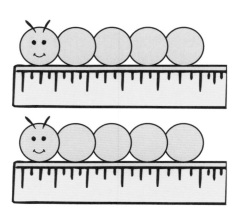

1. Ben's caterpillar was 8 inches long. Kate's caterpillar was 2 inches shorter. Lynn's caterpillar was 3 inches longer than Kate's caterpillar. How long were Kate's and Lynn's caterpillars?

   Kate's caterpillar was _____ inches long.

   Lynn's caterpillar was _____ inches long.

2. Todd's caterpillar was 7 inches long. Rick's caterpillar was 3 inches longer than Todd's. Rick's caterpillar was twice as long as David's. How long were Rick's and David's caterpillars?

   Rick's caterpillar was _____ inches long.

   David's caterpillar was _____ inches long.

3. Ann, Jan, and Fran made caterpillars that were the same length. The girls placed the caterpillars in a line. The line measured 18 inches. How long was each caterpillar?

   Each caterpillar was _____ inches long.

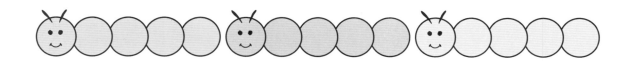

Heavier or Lighter?

Look at each pair of items. Circle the one that is heavier or lighter.

1. Which is heavier?

balloon

basketball

2. Which is lighter?

feather

cup

3. Which is heavier?

bowl

pencil

4. Which is lighter?

spoon

straw

Draw something that is lighter than an apple. Draw something that is heavier than an apple.

lighter than an apple

heavier than an apple

Ounces or Pounds?

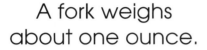

A fork weighs
about one ounce.

A shoe weighs
about one pound.

Write ounces or pounds to show how much each object weighs.
Write the word that makes the most sense.

1.

about 4 _____

3.

about 8 _____

5.

about 2 _____

2.

about 10 _____

4.

about 15 _____

6.

about 2 _____

How Much Time Does It Take?

Name _____

How long would it take to do each activity? Circle the best answer.

1. A child eats a sandwich.

minutes

hours

days

2. A seed grows into a plant.

minutes

hours

days

3. A plane flies across the country.

minutes

hours

days

4. People watch a baseball game.

minutes

hours

days

5. A child builds a block tower.

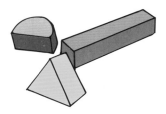

minutes

hours

days

6. Workers build a house.

minutes

hours

days

What is one thing that takes you only a few minutes to do?

_____

What is one thing that takes you over an hour to do?

_____

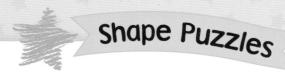

Shape Puzzles

Each shape inside the box can be made by putting together two shapes that are outside the box. Draw a line from each shape inside the box to the two shapes that can be joined together to make it.

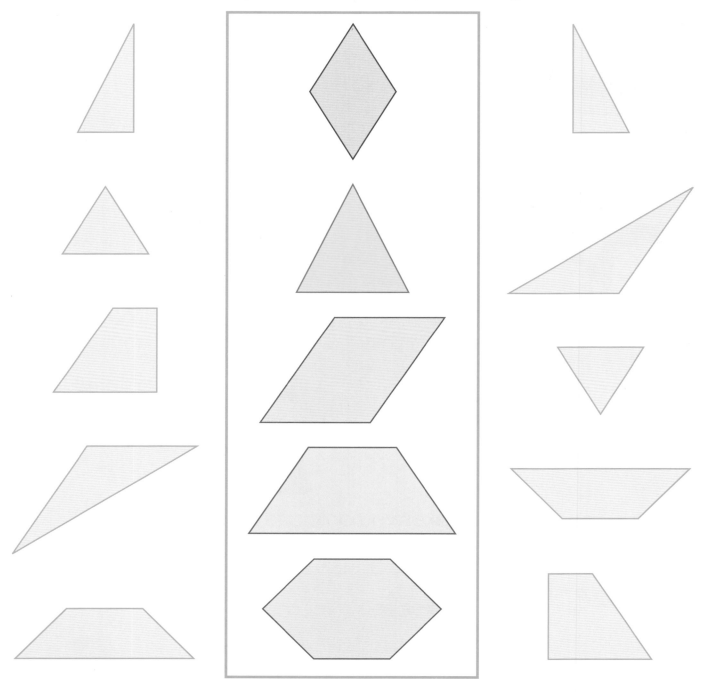

Shape Designs

These children are describing their designs. Write the letters of the matching pictures on the correct lines.

1.  I drew three squares. None of the squares are the same size. _____

2.  I drew three different shapes. None of the shapes touch each other. _____

3.  I drew four triangles that are the same size. I drew two squares that are different sizes. _____

4.  I drew four triangles. The triangles are different sizes. _____

5.  I drew three squares. One square touches the other two squares. _____

6.  I drew three shapes. All three shapes touch one another. _____

A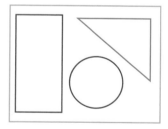

B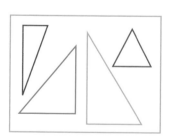

C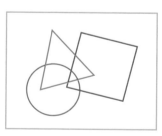

D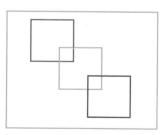

E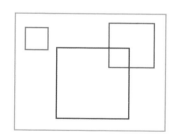

F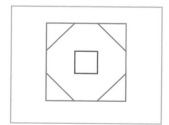

Hidden Squares

Count the total number of squares in each picture.
Watch out for hidden squares!

1.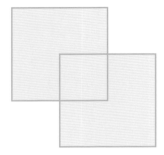

_____ squares

3.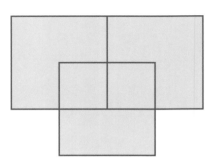

_____ squares

2.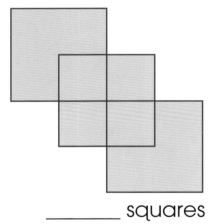

_____ squares

4.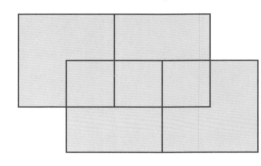

_____ squares

Draw a picture that
has hidden squares.

Name _____

Write how many triangles can be found in each picture.

1.

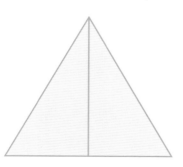

_____ triangles

4.

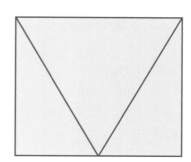

_____ triangles

2.

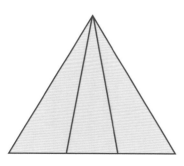

_____ triangles

5.

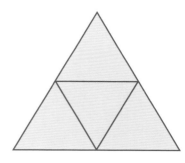

_____ triangles

3.

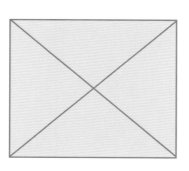

_____ triangles

6.

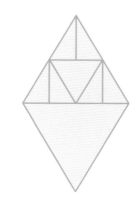

_____ triangles

Paper Cutouts

Look at the six pieces of paper. They were folded in half and a shape was cut out of each one. Write the letters A to E to match the shapes with the paper they were cut from.

1. 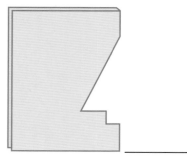 _____

2. 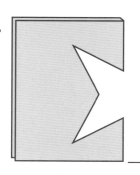 _____

3. 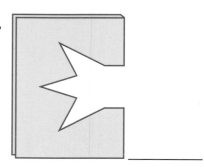 _____

4. 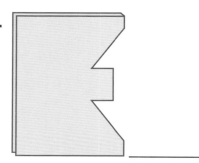 _____

5.  _____

6. 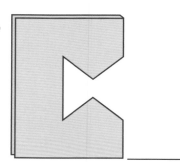 _____

A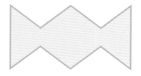

B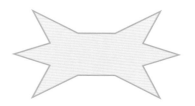

C

D

E

F

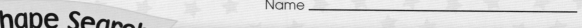

Shape Search

Name _____

Look at the shape in each row. Find it in the design and color it.

1.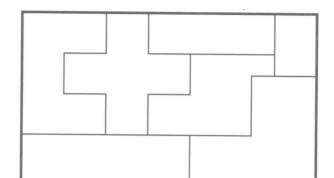

2.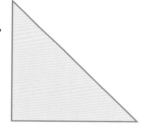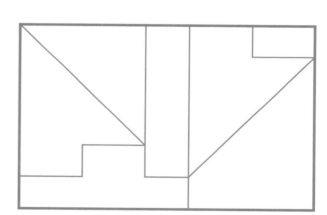

3.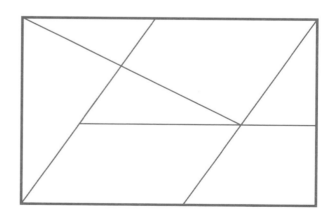

Robot Riddles

Read the riddles. Write the letters of the robots they describe.

1. I have a square head. The rest of me is made of squares or rectangles. _____

2. I have a head shaped like a rectangle. I have five circles on my body. _____

3. My feet are shaped like squares. The rest of me has squares, rectangles, and triangles. _____

4. I have hands and feet made of triangles. I have two circles for each leg. _____

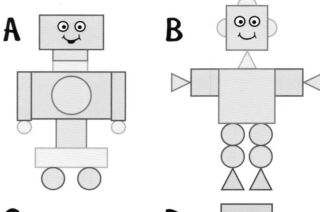

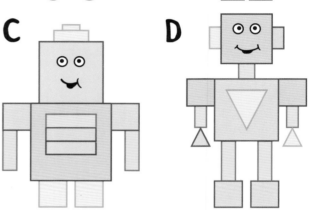

Draw a robot made up of shapes. Write two sentences about your robot.

_____

_____

_____

_____

What's on the Bottom?

Suppose you picked up each object below. What would its base (the bottom part) look like? Write the letter of the matching shape. (You may choose a shape more than once.)

1.

_____

2.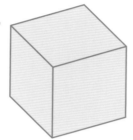

_____

3.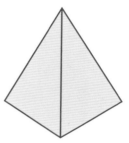

_____

4.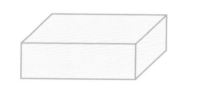

_____

5.

_____

6.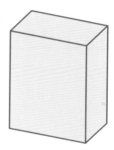

_____

A

square

B

circle

C

rectangle

Look around your home. Find an object with a base shaped like a square. Find an object with a base shaped like a circle. Find an object with a base shaped like a rectangle. List the objects you find.

_____

_____

Color and Count

Find the shapes. Color them. Then write how many shapes you found.

1. Color each △.

How many did you find?

_____

3. Color each ▢.

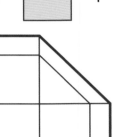

How many did you find?

_____

2. Color each ▱.

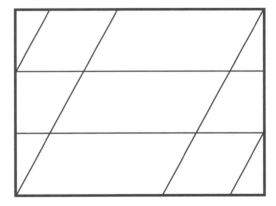

How many did you find?

_____

4. Color each ⏢.

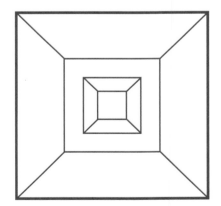

How many did you find?

_____

Cool Scoops

Name _____

Joe's ice cream shop is having a very special sale. Two scoops of ice cream are being sold for the price of one! Joe has sold so much ice cream that he has only three flavors left—chocolate, banana, and cherry.

Color the ice cream scoops brown, yellow, and red to show the different ways Joe can combine the ice cream flavors. (Joe can sell two scoops of one flavor or two scoops of two different flavors.)

Benny's Outfits

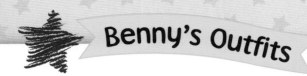

Benny has three shirts. They are green, purple, and red. Benny has three pairs of pants. They are blue, black, and brown. Color the pictures to show how many different outfits Benny can wear.

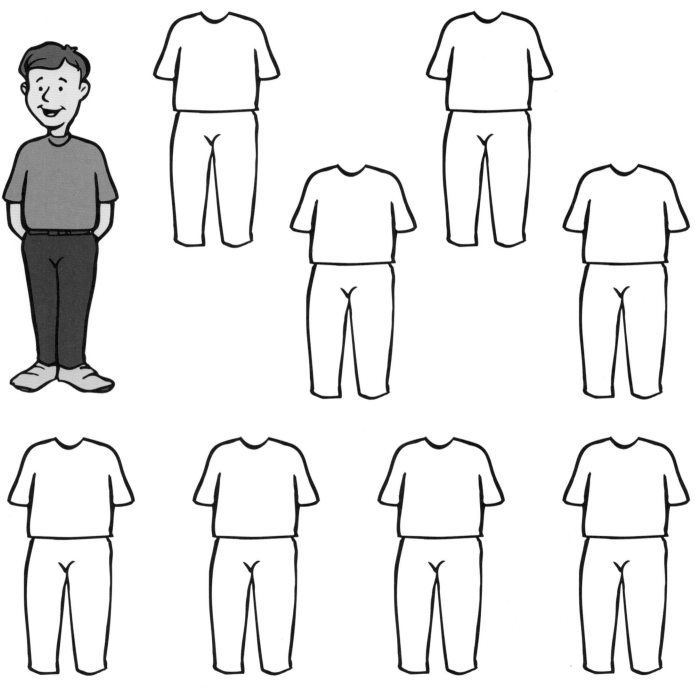

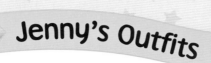

Jenny's Outfits

Name _____

Jenny's favorite colors are red and yellow. She has a red hat, a red T-shirt, and a red pair of shorts. She also has a yellow hat, a yellow T-shirt, and a yellow pair of shorts. Color the pictures to show how many different ways Jenny can mix and match her clothes.

Goldfish Pets

Name _____

Meg   Greg   Sue   Dru

Color the graph to show how many pets each child has. Then answer the questions.

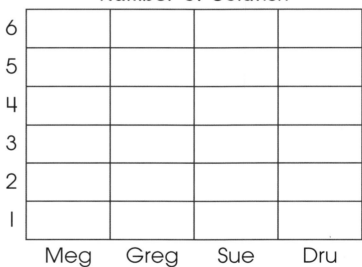

Number of Goldfish

	Meg	Greg	Sue	Dru
6				
5				
4				
3				
2				
1				

1. Who has the most goldfish? _____

2. Who has the fewest goldfish? _____

3. Who has half as many fish as Dru? _____

4. Who has three more fish than Meg? _____

5. How many fish do the four children have altogether? _____

Answer Key—Reading

Page 9

bright   pretty
center   plate
fast   hop
silly   dad

Page 10

scream ill
Synonyms and
sentences will vary.

Page 11

tired, bag, pick, pull,
cut, porch

Page 12

Pictures will vary but
should portray the
opposite of the first
picture.

Page 13

pull: push
fast: slow
thin: fat
break: fix
harm: help
winter: summer
loser: winner

Page 14

light
right
low
quickly
shouted
child
weak
noisy

Page 15

can: A, B
band: A, B
cap: B, A
crow: B, A

Page 16

D   E   A
F   B   C

Page 17

A

B
A
B
A

Page 18

quiet
quite

freight
fright

loose
lose

Page 19

couch
coach

picture
pitcher

guest
guessed

Page 20

late – tired
broke – angry
tutu – silly

Page 21

cold wind, lack of heat
– jacket
small islands – large
vitamins – good
very large, a lot – many

Page 22

yummy
tease
stop
lively
shined
smart

Page 23

tell
understand
little
petted
yelled

Page 25

Jumpin' Jack
Jumpin' Jack had two
pointy white ears, a
black body, and four
white feet that looked
like socks.
He shared his food and
helped baby bunnies
with their hops.
Answers will vary.

Page 26

Interview questions and
answers will vary.

Page 27

Places will vary.

Page 28

It was very hot during
the day and cold at
night.

I would take summer
clothes for during the
day and warmer ones
for night.

No, because the
ground is too dry.

There are no trees to
climb in the desert.

Page 29

The story takes place on
Sunday.

The season is summer.

It is morning.

Page 30

Maps will vary.

Page 31

Answers will vary.

Page 32

Newspaper articles will
vary but should use the
information written on
page 31.

Page 33

nonfiction

fiction

nonfiction

Page 34

fiction

nonfiction

Page 35

3   1
1   3
2   2

Page 36

Page 37

CLIMB UP A TREE AND
ACT LIKE A NUT.

A GARBAGE TRUCK

TO CATCH UP ON HIS
SLEEP

Page 38

1. My cat was hungry.

2. I filled a bowl with
   cat food.

3. My cat was full and
   went to sleep.

1. My teacher gave us a
   list of spelling words.

2. I studied for my
   spelling test.

3. I got a gold star.

Page 39

bowl, spatula, mixer, paper towels, cupcake tin, spoon, cat, milk, girl

Chocolate Attack!

They aren't as clever or as interesting.

Page 40

Asleep for the Winter

Our New Fish

Spring Cleaning

Page 41

Titles will vary.

Page 42

no
yes
yes
no
yes
no
Sentences will vary.

Page 43

1. no
2. no
3. no
4. John and his mother made a fort.

Page 44

girl's baseball cap is turned differently

third flower has 8 petals

Page 45

Cow is a cashier; it's wearing a hat
elephant is in parrot cage
dogfish is not a real fish
mouse is in scuba gear in a fish tank
iguana has braces
the snail is not a dog and should not have a collar

boy in animal cage
gerbil in sneakers
"new kittens" sign points to puppies

Page 46

1. bears, whales, sea otters, moose

2. bug spray, raincoat

3. flamingos, platypuses, lions

Page 47

2. Sally has a lot to learn about caring for her new pet.

1. How to clean its cage

Page 48

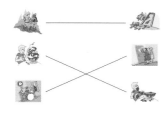

Page 49

Page 50

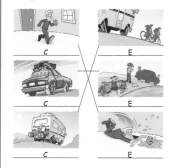

Page 51

Now they have room inside the garage to store Erin's bike.

Frank made the basketball team.

Page 52

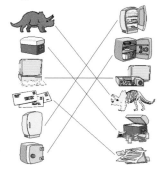

Page 53

Famous Actresses of the Stage, Amazing Animals of the Amazon, Abraham Lincoln's Life, Spend a Day With a Doctor!

Page 54

warm
before
poor
forgetful
school

Page 55

bakery
bookstore
hospital
park

Page 56

crayons
airplane
journal
goggles
music

Page 57

Answer will vary.

Page 58

Pictures will vary but should make sense given the first picture.

Page 59

Pictures will vary.

Page 60

turtle
squirrel
giraffe
skunk
spider
Children should draw pictures of each animal in the box opposite its name.

Page 61

first and second girl
first and third boy
second and third deer
first and second frog

Page 62

scuba divers, fish, seaweed, ocean, bubbles should be circled

Page 63

Justin Jesse Julie Jordan Jackie

Page 64

P	J	C
J	C	P
J	P	C

Page 65

trapeze artist – S
astronaut – S
cook – G
scuba diver – W
mail carrier – G
sailor – S
airline pilot – S
fireman – S or G

Page 66

Pictures will vary.

Answer Key—Writing

Page 67
person – doctor
place – playground
thing – mitten

Page 68
Children should write the name of each noun on the lines provided.

Page 69
lake, crocodile, sneakers, flower, duck, present

Page 70
runs, jumps, hops

Page 71
swings, shouts, hops, catches, rides
Sentences will vary.

Page 72
The second sentence is more interesting.
Adjectives: tiny, special, regular, weird, wonderful, wacky, polka-dotted, rainbow-colored

Page 73
purple, hungry, wiggly, loud, kind, beautiful

Page 74
Pictures and word lists will vary.

Page 75
I ate chocolate brownies.
Tomorrow I am going to the circus.
She plays basketball.
He has lots of freckles.
The elephant is huge and gray.

Page 76
Children should add a period to the end of each sentence.

Page 77
Children should trace and write question marks. They should add

a question mark to the end of each question.

Page 79
On, Tuesday, The Fourth, July, In Hawaii, My, August, Sara, Gabriel, I

Page 80
Sentence endings will vary.

Page 81
Sentence endings will vary.

Page 82
Sentence beginnings will vary.

Page 83
Sentence beginnings will vary.

Page 84
Picture 3 should be first, then Picture 1, then Picture 4, and finally Picture 2.

Page 87
My cousin, Nanuk, invited me to the Arctic. There was lots of snow! We built a huge igloo.

Page 88
I went snorkeling with my friend.
We put on flippers and goggles.
Underwater we saw a giant fish.

Page 89
last, first, next
next, first, last

Page 90
First, Next, Last

Page 91
Pictures and sentences will vary.

Page 92
Story endings will vary.

Page 93
Story endings will vary.

Page 94
Story beginnings and middles will vary.

Page 95
Story beginnings and middles will vary.

Page 96
Stories will vary.

Page 97
Stories will vary.

Page 98
Stories will vary.

Page 99
Stories will vary.

Page 100
Ideas will vary.

Page 101
Stories will vary.

Page 102
Word lists will vary.

Page 103
Stories will vary.

Page 104
Story beginnings will vary.

Page 105
Story beginnings will vary.

Page 106
Story middles will vary.

Page 107
Story middles will vary.

Page 108
Story endings will vary.

Page 109
Story endings will vary.

Page 110
Ideas will vary.

Page 111
Stories will vary.

Page 112
Adjective choices will vary.

Page 113
Adjectives will vary.

Page 115

I love too swim moore than most fissh. Swimming is my favorite sport because i am super goode at it. I kan swim fast. i like to swim in mi pool, but once i swam in the ocean wit my dad. tuesday is pizza day at my school. do you want to come too mi partee? mr. north is taking us to the circus on fridae.

Pages 116 and 117
Stories and illustrations will vary.

Page 118
Answers will vary.

Page 119
Answers will vary.

Page 121
Letters will vary.

Page 122
Stories will vary.

Page 123
Stories and pictures will vary.

Page 124
Stories will vary.

Page 125
Stories and pictures will vary.

Answer Key—Math

Page 127
Numbers left in the box: 6, 14, 18

Page 128

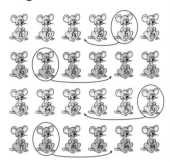

Page 129

Page 130
1. Eric
2. Joni
3. Abby
4. Ryan
5. Todd
6. Becky

Page 131

	12	24	6	3
7	11	5	14	21
18	26	10	2	15
4	13	1	19	17
8	22	16	20	

Numbers should be written as follows: 2, 4, 6, 8, 10, 12, 14, 16, 18, 20, 22, 24, 26.

Page 132

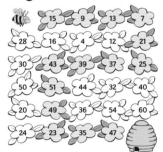

Page 133
1. 32
2. 57
3. 64
4. 27
5. 86
6. 79
7. 82

Pages 134 and 135
1. 11
2. 18
3. 60
4. 35

Clues and mystery number will vary.

Page 136
1. 5
2. 6
3. 7
4. 6
5. 10
6. 9

Page 137
1. 6 + 3 = 11 – 2
2. 5 – 2 = 10 – 7
3. 6 + 2 = 12 – 4
4. 8 + 6 = 9 + 5
5. 12 – 3 = 17 – 8
6. 16 – 8 = 5 + 3
7. 9 + 6 = 8 + 7
8. 11 – 3 = 17 – 9

Page 138

Page 139
Answers will vary. Here are some examples:
1 + 2 + 9 = 12
2 + 4 + 6 = 12
3 + 4 + 5 = 12
2 + 3 + 7 = 12
1 + 2 + 3 + 6 = 12
1 + 2 + 4 + 5 = 12

Page 140
(One way your child might solve the problem is by manipulating pieces of paper that have been numbered 1 to 9. Suggest starting with the numbers that add up to 7—1, 2, 4. Then let your child rearrange the remaining six numbers to figure out the answers for 15 and 23.)

15—3, 5, 7; 7—1, 2, 4; 23—6, 8, 9

Page 141
Balloons should be completed as follows: 1, 6, 8; 4, 2, 9; 5, 7, 3.

Page 142
(If you wish, give your child pieces of colored paper or other objects to work out the problems. In the first problem, your child can take eight pieces of paper and divide them into two equal groups. In the second problem, your child can lay down one piece of red paper and two pieces of yellow paper; your child should keep doing this until he or she gets 12 pieces of paper. In the third problem, your child

can arrange eight pieces of paper into two groups so that one group has four more pieces than the other.)
1. boys—4; girls—4
2. red balloons—4; yellow balloons—8
3. boxes—6; bags—2

Page 143
1. Frankie will land on 10. (He jumps two numbers at a time.)
2. Frankie will land on 12. (He jumps four numbers at a time.)
3. Frankie will land on 9. (He jumps one number, two number, one number, two numbers, and so on.)
4. Frankie will land on 10. (He jumps one number, two numbers, three numbers, four numbers.)

Page 144
1. 15, 18 (Add 3.)
2. 41, 51 (Add 10.)
3. 12, 10 (Subtract 2.)
4. 56, 67 (Add 11.)
5. 54, 44 (Subtract 10.)
6. 11, 16 (Add 1, add 2, add 3, and so on.)

Page 145
Caterpillars should be completed as follows:
1. two lines, one dot
2. dot, triangle
3. three dots, three lines
4. five lines, six lines
5. two lines, one line

Page 146
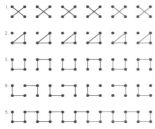
Child's pattern at bottom of page will vary.

Page 147
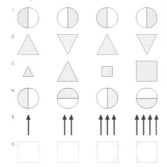

Page 148

Page 149
Coin combinations will vary. There are 13 possible combinations.
1 quarter
2 dimes, 1 nickel
2 dimes, 5 pennies
1 dime, 3 nickels
1 dime, 2 nickels, 5 pennies
1 dime, 1 nickel, 10 pennies
1 dime, 15 pennies
5 nickels
4 nickels, 5 pennies
3 nickels, 10 pennies
2 nickels, 15 pennies
1 nickel, 20 pennies
25 pennies

Page 150
(Your child may wish to lay out real coins to solve these problems.)
1. Coin amounts should be filled out (1¢, 10¢, 1¢, 10¢, and so on). Jack—55¢
2. Coin amounts should be filled out (5¢, 10¢, 1¢, 5¢, 10¢, 1¢, and so on). Lisa—53¢
3. Jack

Page 151
1. whistle, car
2. yo-yo, top, whistle
3. Carl—yo-yo; Lee—whistle

4. 5 whistles; 2 tops and 1 whistle; 1 car and 1 top; 1 car and 2 whistles; 1 yo-yo and 1 whistle

Page 152
1. B, E
2. C, E
3. least amount—15¢; most amount—90¢
4. B, C, E
5. A, D, E

Page 153
Flowers should be colored as follows: 3 red, 2 yellow, 2 purple, 1 orange.

Page 154
(Your child should begin this problem by pairing the purple and yellow bunnies since this is the only possible color combination involving the purple.) The bunnies should be colored as follows: purple and yellow; brown and black; pink and blue.

Page 155
(Your child may want to manipulate red, green, yellow, and brown paper squares to solve the problem.)

The dinosaurs should be colored as follows (from left to right): red, brown, yellow, green.

Page 156
From shortest to tallest—Jed, Ted, Fred, Ed

Page 157

Page 158
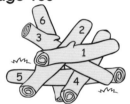

Page 159
Randy's Groups—red shapes, blue shapes
Sandy's Groups—squares, circles
Shapes can be drawn and labeled to show one group with big shapes and the other group with little shapes.

Page 160
One way your child can solve these problems is by reading the information and making a guess.

Then based on the criteria, your child revise his or her guess. For example, suppose your child guesses 3 clowns and 4 horses in the first problem. He or she will determine that though the number of heads is correct, the number of legs is too high; your child will then need to adjust the original guess.
1. clowns—4; horses—3
2. bicycles—3; tricycles—2
3. red balloons—10; blue balloons—5

Page 161
1. E
2. D
3. A
4. B
C is not described.
Suggestions for clues: He has no hat. He has stripes. He has no suspenders.

Page 162
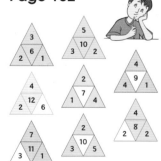

Page 163
round box—6
square box—10

Page 164
1. 3
2. 5
3. 5
4. 3
5. 4
6. 5
7. Dan, Lee, Matt, Jill, Sue, Eric, Toby, Amy

Page 165
Guesses will vary. Actual lengths in inches are as follows:
1. 4
2. 5
3. 3
4. 6

Page 166
1. Kate's caterpillar—6 inches; Lynn's caterpillar—9 inches
2. Rick's caterpillar—10 inches; David's caterpillar—5 inches
3. Each caterpillar was 6 inches long.

Page 167
These pictures should be circled:
1. basketball
2. feather
3. bowl
4. straw
Drawings will vary.

Page 168
1. ounces
2. pounds
3. ounces
4. pounds
5. ounces
6. pounds

Page 169
1. minutes
2. days
3. hours
4. hours
5. minutes
6. days

Answers to questions will vary.

Page 170
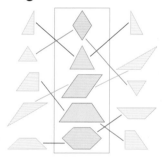

Page 171
1. E
2. A
3. F
4. B
5. D
6. C

Page 172
1. 3
2. 7
3. 5
4. 7

Page 173
1. 3 triangles
2. 6 triangles (3 small triangles, 2 formed by two triangles, one formed by three triangles)
3. 8 triangles (4 small triangles, 4 formed by two triangles)
4. 3 triangles
5. 5 triangles (4 small triangles, 1 formed by four triangles)
6. 12 triangles (6 small triangles, 2 triangles formed by two triangles, 4 triangles formed by three triangles)

Page 174
1. E
2. F
3. B
4. C
5. D
6. A

Page 175
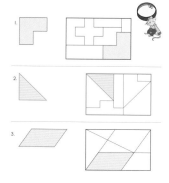

Page 176
1. C
2. A
3. D
4. B

Picture and sentences will vary.

Page 177
1. B
2. A
3. A
4. C
5. B
6. C

List of objects will vary.

Page 178
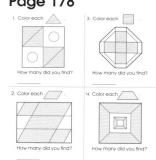
1. 4
2. 5
3. 5
4. 8

Page 179
Ice cream scoops should be colored with these six pairs of colors: brown/brown; yellow/yellow; red/red; brown/yellow; brown/red; yellow/red.

Page 180
T-shirts/pants should be colored with these nine pairs of colors: green/blue; green/black; green/brown purple/blue; purple/black; purple/brown red/blue; red/black; red/brown

Page 181
T-shirt/shorts/hat should be colored with these eight combinations of colors: red/red/red; red/red/yellow; red/yellow/red; red/yellow/yellow yellow/yellow/yellow; yellow/yellow/red; yellow/red/yellow; yellow/red/red

Page 182
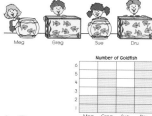
1. Dru
2. Meg
3. Sue
4. Greg
5. 16

Notes